Moral Responsibility, Statecraft, and Humanitarian Intervention

This book explores the moral complexity of statecraft in the context of decision-making on armed intervention in the post-Cold War era. It adds to the debate on humanitarian intervention by analyzing the moral complexity of statecraft when confronted with situations of severe human rights violations. Through a comparative case study of the Clinton administration's failure to intervene in the Rwanda genocide (1994), the George W. Bush administration's tepid response to the Darfur atrocities (2003–2007), and the Barack Obama administration's leadership behind the limited UN intervention in Libya (2011), it explores the factors – domestic and international – that influence decision-making about humanitarian intervention. These cases show not only how international moral concerns often compete with interest-based and domestic concerns, but how decision-makers are often confronted by competing moral imperatives. In such situations, it is often not clear which imperatives should be followed.

In an increasingly interconnected world, *Moral Responsibility, Statecraft, and Humanitarian Intervention* examines how we expect state leaders to balance different moral responsibilities. It will be of much interest to students of humanitarian intervention, the Responsibility to Protect, human rights, US foreign policy, African politics and IR in general.

Cathinka Vik is an Associate Professor in the Department of Health, Technology and Society at Gjovik University College, Norway, and has a PhD in International Relations from the University of Miami.

Global Politics and the Responsibility to Protect

Series editors:
Alex J. Bellamy (Griffith University), Sara E. Davies (Griffith University) and Monica Serrano (The City University of New York)

The aim of this book series is to gather the best new thinking about the responsibility to protect into a core set of volumes to provide a definitive account of the principle, its implementation, and its role in crises, while reflecting a plurality of views and regional perspectives.

Global Politics and the Responsibility to Protect
From words to deeds
Alex J. Bellamy

The Responsibility to Protect
Norms, laws and international politics
Ramesh Thakur

Humanitarian Intervention and the Responsibility to Protect
Security and human rights
Cristina G. Badescu

Sri Lanka and the Responsibility to Protect
Politics, ethnicity, genocide
Damien Kingsbury

International Responsibility and Grave Humanitarian Crises
Collective provision for human security
Hannes Peltonen

Global Justice, Kant and the Responsibility to Protect
A provisional duty
Heather M. Roff

Moral Responsibility, Statecraft, and Humanitarian Intervention

The US response to Rwanda, Darfur, and Libya

Cathinka Vik

Routledge
Taylor & Francis Group

LONDON AND NEW YORK

First published 2015
by Routledge
2 Park Square, Milton Park, Abingdon, Oxon OX14 4RN

and by Routledge
711 Third Avenue, New York, NY 10017

Routledge is an imprint of the Taylor & Francis Group, an informa business

British Library Cataloguing-in-Publication Data
A catalogue record for this book is available from the British Library

Library of Congress Cataloging-in-Publication Data
Vik, Cathinka.
Moral responsibility, statecraft, and humanitarian intervention : the US
response to Rwanda, Darfur, and Libya / Cathinka Vik.
pages cm. — (Global politics and the responsibility to protect)
Includes bibliographical references and index.
1. United States—Foreign relations—1989—Moral and ethical aspects.
2. Humanitarian intervention—Rwanda. 3. Humanitarian intervention—
Sudan—Darfur. 4. Humanitarian intervention—Libya. 5. Rwanda—
History—Civil War, 1994. 6. Sudan—History—Darfur Conflict, 2003-
7. Libya—History—Civil War, 2011– I. Title.
JZ1480.V55 2015
172'.4—dc23
2014047663

ISBN: 978-1-138-88799-2 (hbk)
ISBN: 978-1-315-71376-2 (ebk)

Typeset in Times by
FiSH Books Ltd, Enfield

Printed and bound in the United States of America by Edwards Brothers
Malloy on sustainably sourced paper.

The book is dedicated to my beloved husband, Jan Tore,
and to our dear family,
with gratitude for their kind and compassionate hearts.

Contents

Acknowledgements

This book is directly attributable to the insight, encouragement, and feedback of many people. Above all, I am indebted to my parents, Elisabeth and Thor Henning, whose example, vision, and unconditional love have motivated this work. I am forever grateful to my beloved husband, Jan Tore, and to my beautiful sisters, Martine, Karoline and Kari, for their perpetual unbound affection and hope showered upon me.

The topic of this book was conceived during my time as a student at the University of Miami. I would like to thank my supervisors at the time for their insight, support, and encouragement, without which the foundation for this book would not have been written. I am especially grateful to Ruth Reitan for her constant support and encouragement. Her constructive criticism and patient push stretched my understanding of this topic. Special thanks are also due to Henrik Syse for inspiring me to continuously strive for knowledge in service to humanity, and for his crucial role in my professional development and in the development of this book. I would also like to acknowledge and extend my heartfelt gratitude to Ambler Moss, Laura Gomez-Mera, and Roger Kanet, for their invaluable input in the earlier stages of the writing process.

Initially written as a dissertation, this manuscript demanded time, feedback, and effort to transform into a publishable book. The transformation of the draft version into this final manuscript is the result of the thorough, thoughtful and constructive comments provided by series editor Alex Bellamy, and by the anonymous reviewers. I am deeply grateful for the time and energy they devoted into critically reading the manuscript and suggesting substantial improvements. In its current format, the book owes its existence to the support of my colleagues at Gjovik University College. In particular, I thank Heidi Vifladt and Roger Lian for giving me the opportunity and time to produce this work.

Although many people provided input on the content on this book, the mistakes of fact and judgment are mine alone. I have done my best to tell the story accurately and fairly, and I welcome comments and criticism from readers that can help me improve my work.

Finally, it would be impossible to adequately acknowledge here the many other people who have contributed to this book in various ways. My heartfelt gratitude goes to all my friends around the world for teaching me, through example, the importance and power of love and sacrifice in developing ties of friendships across political and cultural boundaries.

Introduction

This book explores the moral complexity of statecraft in the context of decision-making on armed intervention in the post-Cold War era. The genocides in Rwanda (1994) and Srebrenica (1995) raised questions about the moral legitimacy of states ravaged by human rights violations, and about the responsibility of outside states to protect innocent civilians from being massacred across political and cultural boundaries. In this context, the concept of humanitarian intervention as an expression of international moral responsibility emerged as one of the most controversial foreign policy issues of our time, highlighting the complexity of moral decision-making in international relations.[1]

The concept of humanitarian intervention implies that there exists a moral responsibility on behalf of some actor or actors to protect innocent civilians from massacre in situations where the state fails in its responsibility to do so. Yet if "states are now widely understood to be instruments at the service of their peoples, and not vice versa" (Annan 1999: n.p.), a question emerges as to how this affects the moral decision-making of potential intervening states. While there is universal agreement that, in the face of genocide, "something must be done," the idea that states refusing to commit troops to end such atrocities are morally bereft is not axiomatic.

According to the United Nations Charter, the primary responsibility for the maintenance of international peace and security rests with the UN Security Council. Article 24 of the Charter affirms that member-states "confer on the Security Council primary responsibility for the maintenance of international peace and security, and agree that in carrying out its duties under this responsibility the Security Council acts in their behalf" (UN 1948). The members of the UN Security Council likewise pledge "to accept and carry out the decisions of the Security Council" (*ibid.*: Article 25). Correspondingly, the active participation of the permanent members of the UN Security Council is crucial to the implementation of coherent and consistent responses to situations of severe human rights violations. Owing to this structure, Stevenson declared in an address to the Chicago Bar Association in 1945 (quoted in Schlesinger 2003: 261) that "everything depends on the active participation, pacific intentions and good faith of the Big Five." With this, the international community has left the responsibility of protecting humanity's interests in the hands of state leaders elected to protect the lives and promote the interests of their respective populations. A problem thus emerges, as Tim Dunne (2003) warns, that the anti-hegemonial character of international society is threatened by an enforced hierarchy rooted in a unilateralist conception of interest appealing to a Hobbesian model of international politics. In such a climate of international politics, state leaders find themselves struggling to reconcile their pluralist (national) and solidarist (international) commitments. Accordingly, humanitarian intervention – essentially an expression of solidarist moral sentiment, risks becoming the hypocritical rhetorical window-dressing that realists and other cynics have typically dismissed it as (Williams 2005).

This book adds to the debate on humanitarian intervention by analyzing the moral complexity of state leadership when confronted with situations of severe human rights violations. Through a comparative case study of the US President Bill Clinton administration's failure to intervene in the Rwanda genocide (1994), the George W. Bush administration's tepid response to the Darfur atrocities (2003–2007), and the Barack Obama administration's leadership behind the limited UN intervention in Libya (2011), it explores the factors – domestic and international – that influence decision-making about humanitarian intervention. The cases show not only how international moral concerns often compete with interest-based and domestic concerns, but how decision-makers are often confronted by competing moral imperatives. In such situations, it is often not clear which imperatives should be followed. This is especially true when the question at stake is one of military intervention, where the outcomes are so difficult to predict with any certainty.

By examining the moral complexity of state leadership, this book suggests that in order to gain a clearer understanding of the concept of moral responsibility in international relations, the moral stance of states and policy-makers must be separated from the moral stance of individuals. In this sense, this book corroborates Machiavelli's famous argument:

> It must be understood, however, that a prince ... cannot observe all of those virtues for which men are reputed good, because it is often necessary to act against mercy, against faith, against humanity, against frankness, against religion in order to preserve the state. Thus he must be disposed to change according as the winds of fortune and the alternations of circumstance dictate. ... he must stick to the good so long as he can, but being compelled by necessity, he must be ready to take the way of evil ...
>
> (Machiavelli 1984: 93)

Yet this is not to suggest that the complexity of statecraft excuses inaction in response to situations of genocide. On the contrary, this book argues that an international community serious about the pledge of "never again" must address this complexity in order to avoid continued inconsistencies in response to mass atrocities. In order to secure consistent responses to situations of severe human rights violations, therefore, the unique ethical sphere of statecraft must be addressed.

The United States has been selected as a focus in this study for two reasons. As the strongest member of the Security Council in the Cold War-era, the United States has been essential to any large-scale humanitarian initiative. It thus plays a particularly important role in decision-making on armed intervention. Moreover, as acknowledged by Obama (2011), the United States has historically been among the strongest proponents of the diffusion of cosmopolitan values through military intervention: "For generations, the United States of America has played a unique role as an anchor of global security and advocate for human freedom."

Yet in three similar cases of severe human rights violations – Rwanda, Darfur, and Libya – the United States failed to intervene adequately to protect an estimated number of between 700,000 and 1,450,000 civilians from being massacred.[2] The cases of Rwanda, Darfur, and Libya therefore seem to indicate that national self-interest continues to prevail over humanitarian concerns in international relations. How do these cases inform our understanding of the state as a moral actor and the notion of moral responsibility in international relations?

The genocide in Rwanda was one of the most intensive killing campaigns in human history. On 6 April 1994, President Habyarimana's plane was shot down as it approached Kigali airport, sparking the implementation of a "final solution" to the Tutsi "problem" in Rwanda. Within two weeks, an estimated 800,000 Tutsis and moderate Hutus were hacked to death with machetes, with breathtaking rapidity. It was the first unequivocal case of genocide since the Holocaust, with a "daily killing rate" of "at least five times that of the Nazi death camps" (Prunier 1995: 261). By the end of April, "half of the Tutsi population of Rwanda" had been murdered (Human Rights Watch 1999).

The warnings of the impending genocide in Rwanda were countless and clear, providing the international community with an opportunity to confirm its commitment to the pledge of "never again" embedded in the UN Genocide Convention (UN 1951). Yet all major international actors – policy-makers in Belgium, the US, France, and the UN – failed to heed the warnings of the pending disaster and refused to recognize the genocide when it began. They withdrew troops that could have saved lives and avoided the term "genocide" in fear that it would impel decisive action (*ibid.*).

The Rwanda case reveals the rhetoric and idiosyncrasies involved in foreign policy decision-making and the US government's troubled attempt to reconcile its pluralist and solidarist values and commitments. Yet both the avoidance and paralysis characterizing the international community during the genocide in Rwanda, and the subsequent regret – ascertaining the need to strengthen the framework for collective international security responses to mass atrocities – had significant impact on the understanding of the state as a moral actor in international relations. The case of Rwanda is a crucial case because it is the clearest situation in which the moral responsibility to protect populations from genocide stipulated in the UN Genocide Convention would apply in the post-Cold War era.

Aptly, Darfur, on the other hand, has been termed "the ambiguous genocide" (Prunier 2007). In contrast to Rwanda, the international community struggled to reach consensus on whether or not the conflict in Darfur rightfully constituted genocide. Despite this ambiguity, President George W. Bush was quick to invoke the term "genocide," framing the call to respond within the language of the responsibility to protect, which was gaining increased recognition in international discourse at the time. However, despite the president's bold assertion, the US vacillated in its response, failing to hold the government of Sudan accountable for the estimated death toll of 400,000 people in Darfur.

Significantly, and in contrast to the Clinton administration ten years earlier, the Bush administration did not understand the invocation of the term "genocide" to imply an obligation to intervene. Instead this discourse was invoked to accommodate demands by the Christian right and encourage other UN member-states to act. Moreover, the international political climate at the time enabled the Bush administration to couple rhetoric on genocide with a moral responsibility to protect without having to risk intervention in a conflict posing little threat to American interests. Providing cover for the Bush administration's incoherence between words and action, the UN Commission of Inquiry on Darfur (2005) concluded that genocide had not taken place in Darfur. In the case of Darfur, therefore, the US government succeeded in achieving two seemingly contradictory goals: avoiding engagement as well as the stigma associated with standing by while genocide unfolds.

The fact that Clinton was cognizant of an emerging solidarist understanding of international morality and thus did not call a genocide by its rightful name while W. Bush employed the term yet ignored the accompanying responsibility to respond, confirms the US government's continued struggle to reconcile its pluralist and solidarist commitments. It seems to suggest that the solidarist understanding of international moral responsibility advanced by the failure to intervene in Rwanda diminished during the George W. Bush era. Yet, as Badescu and Weiss (2010) point out, misguided justifications and attempted breaches of an emerging ideal may be rejected and "back-fire" to generate the opposite effect. In this manner, the discordant US response to Darfur contributed to clarifying matters and fostering a solidarist expanded notion of moral responsibility in international relations.

In contrast to both Rwanda and Darfur, the UN response to the upheavals in Libya in February 2011 was immediate. The international community's swift response was acclaimed a victory for solidarism. However, Gaddafi's continued violent crackdown in response to the rebellion cast serious doubt on the international community's willingness to sacrifice financial and human resources to prevent further human rights violations. Moreover, the lack of response to the similar situation in Syria raised questions about the sincerity of the international community's solidarist commitment to the UN Genocide Convention and responsibility to protect.

The US justified the American-led intervention by claiming that it was in "the national interest" of the United States to stop a potential massacre that would have "stained the conscience of the world." Emphasizing burden-sharing in humanitarian intervention, the Obama administration substantiated the George W. Bush rhetoric during Darfur by underscoring the moral responsibility to act, while encouraging others to effectuate the obligation. By engaging its complex environment and dual moral commitment, the Obama administration placated domestic concerns by justifying humanitarian intervention in the language of the national interest. With an approach to "saving strangers" that cohered with American national interests, the US response to Libya reinforced the state as a pluralist moral actor while advancing a solidarist commitment within the constraints of a pluralist world.

Arising from a wide range of social, political, economic, and technological forces, a solidarist consciousness has developed in international relations, making a retreat to pluralist state-based conceptions of international order and justice impossible. However, the cases in this study show that attempts to move towards promoting a more consistent and coherent conception of global justice are constrained by the context in which they must develop, which remains heavily structured around pluralist mechanisms that reflect various types of inequality. This tension – and the struggle to reconcile pluralist and solidarist commitments – is reflected in the inconsistent US responses to the cases of severe human rights violations discussed in this study.

This book is structured as follows. Chapter 1 outlines the framework for analysis employed in this study. Chapters 2–4 explore three consecutive presidencies and their responses to situations of severe human rights violations on the African continent in the post-Cold War era. By comparing the nature of, and moral justifications for, the US response, as post-Cold War hegemon, to the atrocities in Rwanda (1994), Darfur (2003–2007), and Libya (2011), these chapters reveal the presidents' struggles to reconcile the United States' pluralist and solidarist commitments. Examined in context, each of these cases discloses the contradictions inherent in the international system, generating inconsistent responses to mass atrocities. The concluding chapter reflects on the three cases, analyzing the factors that influence decision-making on armed intervention in the US, and drawing out its implications for the state as a moral actor in international relations.

Notes

1   Humanitarian intervention refers to the use or threat of coercive (military) means inside the territory of a sovereign state against its will by another state, or a group of other states, with the aim to protect people who suffer severe harm in that state, whereby the performance of the intervention itself needs to be in accordance with humanitarian standards (Schramme 2001).
2   Due to the political, religious, and ethnic biases or prejudices often leading to downplayed or exaggerated figures, determining the number of persons killed in genocide can be difficult. Estimates suggest that between 500,000 and 1,000,000 were killed during the 1994 genocide in Rwanda (OAU 1998; BBC 2004 gives an estimate of 800,000). Between 178,258 (Degomme and Guha-Sapir 2010) and 400,000 (USA Today 2006) are estimated to have been killed in the Darfur conflict between 2003 and

2010. Estimates of deaths in the 2011 Libyan civil war vary from 2,000 to 30,000 between March 2 and September 8 (RT News Line 2011; Associated Press 2011).

References

Annan, K. (1999) Two Concepts of Sovereignty. *The Economist*, 18 September. Available at www.economist.com/node/324795 (accessed 12 January 2015).

Associated Press (2011) Libyan Estimate: At Least 30,000 Died in the War. 8 September. Available at www.sfgate.com/cgi-bin/article.cgi?f=/n/a/2011/09/08/international/i004907D85.DTL (accessed 9 September 2011).

Badescu, C. and Weiss, T. (2010) Misrepresenting R2P and Advancing Norms: An Alternative Spiral? *International Studies Perspective* 11: 354–374.

BBC (2004) Frustration of Darfur "Observer." 14 November. Available at http://news.bbc.co.uk/1/hi/programmes/panorama/4007117.stm (accessed 12 January 2015).

Degomme, O. and Guha-Sapir, D. (2010) Patterns of Mortality Rates in Darfur Conflict. *The Lancet* 375(9711). Available at www.thelancet.com/journals/lancet/article/PIIS0140-6736%2809%2961967-X/abstract (accessed 12 February 2011).

Dunne, T. (2003) Society and Hierarchy in International Relations. *International Relations* 17(3): 303–320.

Human Rights Watch (1999) *Leave None to Tell the Story: Genocide in Rwanda*. New York: Human Rights Watch.

Machiavelli, N. (1984) *The Prince* (trans. D. Donno). New York: Bantam Books.

OAU (1998) OAU Sets Inquiry into Rwanda Genocide. *Africa Recovery* 12(1): 4. Available at www.un.org/ecosocdev/geninfo/afrec/subjindx/121rwan.htm (accessed 11 February 2010).

Obama, B. (2011) Remarks by the President to the Nation on Libya, National Defense University, Washington, DC. 28 March. Available at www.whitehouse.gov/the-press-office/2011/03/28/remarks-president-address-nation-libya (accessed 4 April 2011).

Prunier, G. (2007) *Darfur: The Ambiguous Genocide?*, 2nd edn. Ithaca, NY: Cornell University Press.

—— (1995) *The Rwanda Crisis: History of a Genocide, 1959–1994*. Kampala: Fountain Publishers.

RT News Line (2011) 2 March, 2011. Available at http://rt.com/news/line/2011-03-02 (accessed 9 September 2011).

Schlesinger, S.C. (2003) *Act of Creation: The Founding of the United Nations*. Boulder, CO: Westview Press.

Schramme, T. (2001) Tainted Humanity: The Dilemma of Military Intervention. Available at www.eurozine.com/article/2001-04-01-schramme-en.html (accessed 20 October 2007).

UN (1951). Convention on the Prevention and Punishment of the Crime of Genocide. Adopted by Resolution 260 (III) of the UN General Assembly (9 December 1948). UN Treaty Series no. 1021, 78(277). Available at www.preventgenocide.org/law/convention/text.htm (accessed 6 September 2009).

—— (1948) Charter of the United Nations. Available at www.un.org/en/documents/charter/index.shtml (accessed 12 January 2015).

UN Commission of Inquiry on Darfur (2005) *Report of the International Commission of Inquiry on Darfur to the United Nations Secretary-General.* 25 January. Geneva: United Nations. Available at www.un.org/News/dh/sudan/com_inq_darfur.pdf (accessed 17 November 2010).

USA Today (2006) Debate Over Darfur Death Tolls Intensifies. *USA Today*, 29 November. Available at www.usatoday.com/news/world/2006-11-29-darfur_x.htm (accessed 6 July 2010).

Williams, J. (2005) Pluralism, Solidarism and the Emergence of World Society in English School Theory. *International Relations* 19(1): 19–38.

1 The moral dimension of statecraft

> Whether we can conceive of a way to think of morality that extends some form of sympathy further than our own group remains perhaps the fundamental moral question of contemporary life.
>
> (Jean Tronto 1993: 59)

The academic analysis of moral responsibility in international relations has approached the topic based on three principal conceptions of international morality. The first, international moral skepticism, holds that moral judgments are appropriate only within sovereign political communities and thus denies entirely the intelligibility of moral discourse in international relations.[1] Second, the morality of states or pluralist notion of international morality conceives of international relations as a moral order in the sense that states have obligations to conform to moral rules derived from a "domestic morality analogy," in which international society is understood as a larger domestic society, and where states play the roles occupied by individuals in domestic society.[2] The third, cosmopolitan or solidarist conception of morality, opens up the state to external moral assessment, understanding persons, rather than states, as the ultimate and equal subjects of international morality.[3]

Humanitarian interventions challenge these conceptions of morality in international relations, with most analysis focusing on whether state sovereignty or individual human rights should take precedence in situations where a choice between the two has to be made. Today, it is widely accepted that since "state sovereignty" is an instrumental and not an intrinsic value, "tyranny and anarchy cause the moral collapse of sovereignty" (Tesón 2003: 93). The research on humanitarian intervention and state sovereignty has been invaluable in establishing the individual as the primary object of security in international relations.

However, what this literature has largely failed to consider are the difficulties associated with this solidarist development for governments of potential intervening countries, whose primary moral duty remains the protection of their own citizens. For potential intervening states, the question is not only one of whether individual human rights or state sovereignty should take precedence in situations where a choice between the two has to be made, but one of whether sacrificing the lives of national soldiers to protect the lives of civilians abroad can be vindicated domestically and internationally.

One of the problems inherent in current approaches to humanitarian intervention is that they tend to collapse individual and state morality. Acting on the ideological reservoir of the state, policy makers are at constant risk of losing moral authority by basing their decisions on precedence considerations in situations where their individual moral compass may not be compatible with state policy. Moreover, state leaders must constantly strive to uphold the state's – at times incompatible – domestic and international commitments. Due to the moral complexity of state leadership, therefore, this book suggests that the moral stance of policy-makers must be separated from the moral stance of individuals. Through comparative case studies of the nature of, and moral justifications for, the US response to the atrocities in Rwanda (1994), Darfur (2003–2007), and Libya (2011), this book examines the "unique ethical sphere" of state leadership.

In doing so, this study utilizes a combined English School–relational constructivist framework, adding a theoretical dimension to the literature on humanitarian intervention that is too often underplayed or appears in a one-dimensional way. The English School is useful in this context because it offers an account of international relations that captures the interplay between:

- morality and power;
- the empirical and the normative;
- the national (pluralist) and the international (solidarist);
- order and justice; and
- theory and history (Dunne 2008).

Moreover, it offers insight into dynamics such as the relationship between agency and structure; the orientations of insiders versus outsiders; changes in sovereignty and international legitimacy; and the possible transformation of international society into some kind of world society (Bull 1977; Suganami 1989; Linklater 1998). It thus provides a holistic framework for analyzing the most central question of any normative international theory, namely the moral value to be attributed to particularistic political collectivities against humanity taken as a whole, or the claims of individual human beings (Brown 2009).

Constructivism highlights how these values change over time by providing a framework for analyzing how "logics of appropriateness" evolve in terms of which moral values take precedence in the international system. Within this context of evolving "logics of appropriateness," the relational constructivist emphasis on legitimation through ongoing contestation and rhetorical struggle illuminates key features of the US response to the situations of mass atrocities in Rwanda, Darfur, and Libya, providing new insights into the state as a moral actor and the notion of moral responsibility in international relations. In addition to the above, the analysis of US foreign policy traditions provides a historical context within which the complexity of moral decision-making by state actors in international relations can be explored.

The moral dimension of statecraft in the English School

Drawn from E.H. Carr's (1939) famous antithesis between "reality" (politics) and "utopia" (ethics), a prevailing inclination of international relations scholarship during the second half of the twentieth century was to represent politics and ethics as mutually exclusive spheres (Nardin 2008). According to Carr, "the world of nature," dominated by power, differs from "the world of value," guided by principles of morality. The latter he portrayed as a kind of dream world with little, if any, contact with reality. This "realist" thinking represented by Carr's antithesis is misleading because it poses a bifurcation, which Carr acknowledges at the end of his book:

> If, however, it is utopia to ignore the element of power, it is an unreal kind of realism which ignores the element of morality in any world order. Just as within the state every government, though it needs power as a basis of its authority, also needs the moral basis of the consent of the governed, so an international order cannot be based on power alone, for the simple reason that mankind will in the long run always revolt against naked power. Any international order presupposes a substantial measure of general consent.
>
> (Carr 1939: 235–239)

In Carr's view, therefore, "political action must be based on a coordination of morality and power" (*ibid.*: 97). Realism fails, in Carr's analysis, precisely because it excludes essential features of politics like emotional appeal to a political goal and grounds for moral judgment. R.H. Jackson (2000) similarly acknowledges that in relations between human beings, including in relations among representatives of states in international relations, there is not a choice between the instrumental and the normative, between power and morality. One cannot contemplate the use of power, or actually use power, without justifying it in some way. "Politics and ethics are coupled, and they are both part of the real world" (*ibid.*: 8). Thus, while it is commonly assumed that international relations is a sphere of hypocrisy and power politics, this assumption is misleading because when power is employed in human relations it has to be justified, and most of the controversy surrounding the use of power is whether or not it can be vindicated (*ibid.*: 20). As pointed out by classical realist Hans Morgenthau (cited by Jackson, *ibid.*: 9), "Let me say ... in criticism to those who deny that moral principles are applicable to international politics, that all human actions in some way are subject to moral judgment. We cannot act but morally because we are men." Yet it does not necessarily follow that domestic and international conceptions of moral legitimacy always coincide.

At the heart of the politics of protection debate lies the question "protection of whom?" Concern has in recent decades shifted from states to individuals, groups and communities. In this process, article 1(1) of the UN Charter has been reinterpreted to include security beyond the state, expanding the United Nations mandate to preserve human security as an aspect of "international peace and security" (UN 1948). With this, the distinction between nationals and foreigners traditionally providing the foundation for security in international relations has been challenged significantly. The English School pluralist–solidarist debate, providing "differing judgments about the extent of solidarity or potential solidarity in international society" (Suganami 2002: 13) offers a useful framework for analyzing this question in the context of decision-making on armed intervention.

Solidarism rests on the philosophical normative foundation of cosmopolitanism.[4] In the realms of social and political philosophy, cosmopolitanism is considered the idea that all human beings belong to a single moral community; one which exists regardless of social circumstances, and to which universal moral principles apply (Fienberg 1996). The pluralist argument, in contrast, delineates the international scene into geographic communities (states), which formulate the individual's morality, in a social rather than natural context. For pluralists, the nation state is considered a community whose members are bound by strong ties of solidarity from which moral feelings and a sense of ethical obligation naturally derive (Hoffman 1981). Pluralists thus appeal to particularistic foundations of morality, viewing the state as "the framework that founds and enables the ethical discourse in which social judgments are possible" (Cochran 1995: 48). Without the existence of a higher authority analogous to the state, this framework does not exist at the international level. Instead, the security dilemma generates interactions derived from considerations of interest and fear, and ties of solidarity consequently exist only among states, rather than among individuals regardless of borders (Hoffman 1981).[5] From the pluralist perspective, states, rather than individuals, are thus the main subjects of international morality, and the rules that regulate state behavior are assumed to preserve a peaceful order of sovereign states.[6]

As the world has become a smaller place through increased social, political, and economic contacts, the disputes between cosmopolitan and pluralist arguments, particularly in relation to their different emphases placed on the role of the nation state as a moral actor, and the issues raised by these disputes, have become increasingly apparent. Defenders of solidarism highlight that the development of international norms and organizations, paralleled with steadily increasing economic interdependence, have challenged the nation state's both moral and practical impetus to exist (Beitz 1979). Pluralists, in contrast, maintain that since it conceives of the state as "a manifestation of the community" possessing moral value, globalization does not affect their basic argument (Fienberg 1996).[7]

Applied to situations of prospective humanitarian interventions, the root of this moral controversy relates to the extent and depth of moral obligations to other human beings, extending across political and cultural boundaries. Since state leaders are not morally obliged to weigh the interests of all people equally, pluralists discourage any violation of the principle of state sovereignty, insisting that during wartime, the self-interest of a nation masquerades as a moral cause weighty enough to justify the annihilation of innocent people.[8] In this view, states apply principles of humanitarian intervention selectively, resulting in inconsistency in policy. For pluralists, moral principles do not determine political behavior in the international sphere and can therefore not be used as justification for the violation of another state's right to sovereignty and self-determination (Donnelly 2000). On the contrary, since the international system is a world of conflict and competition in which any nation that practices altruism does so at the expense of its own citizens, altruism by nation states is considered an immoral act that violates the trust that their citizens put in them (Morgenthau, in McElroy 1992: 27). Further, proponents of this view are concerned that in the absence of consensus on what principles should govern a right of humanitarian intervention, the most powerful states would be free to impose their own culturally determined moral values on weaker members of international society.

Solidarists, on the other hand, point to our common humanity to argue that all individuals have basic rights and duties to uphold the rights of others (Caney 1997: 34). In this view, today's globalized world is so integrated that massive human rights violations in one part of the world have an effect on every other part (Blair 1999). In prospective cases of humanitarian intervention, therefore, even where the economic interests and integrity of individual nation states are not in jeopardy, solidarists argue that a broader set of vital interests on behalf of humanity may be involved. Advocates of solidarism argue that the duty to offer charity to those in need is universal (Ramsey 2002: 35–36), and that this is based on moral agreement between the world's major religions and ethical systems that genocide and mass killing are great wrongs that others have a duty to prevent (Lepard 2002).[9]

However, pluralists agree that the international community has a duty to prevent mass killings. Michael Walzer (2000) argues that in extreme cases, what he terms "emergencies" of the magnitude of genocide; acts that "shock the moral conscience of mankind," intervention in the affairs of another state can be justified. Bringing coherence to the pluralist–solidarist debate, Walzer's considerations lower the threshold for humanitarian intervention, recognizing that self-determination is a contingent value, and consequently that, in the face of terror and massacre, the international community does have a moral obligation to stop the killing of innocent people:

> Yes, the norm is not to intervene in other people's countries; the norm is self-determination. But not for these people, the victims of tyranny, ideological zeal, ethnic hatred, who are not determining anything for themselves, who urgently need help from the outside. And it isn't enough to wait until the tyrants, the zealots, and the bigots have done their filthy work and then rush food and medicine to the ragged survivors. Whenever the filthy work can be stopped it should be stopped. And if not by us, the supposedly decent people of the world, then by whom?

> (Walzer 1995: 65)

Walzer's argument demonstrates a fluidity or blending of pluralism and solidarism regarding the question of how far moral responsibility extends in international relations.

The present book proposes that the controversy surrounding the concept of humanitarian intervention in recent decades are reflective of an international community striving to reconcile its pluralist and solidarist commitments. In doing so, this study illustrates English School pluralism and solidarism, not as opposite positions, but rather as coexisting dimensions of an international order within which tensions arise (Almeida 2003). Thus, while recognizing the differences between the two positions, it discards the "zero-sum"-interpretations of the pluralist–solidarist debate (Buzan 2004: 46), inhibiting dialogue between the two camps.

The moral dimension of statecraft in constructivism

Adding to the pluralistic approach of the English School, this study utilizes relational constructivism to provide new insights into the constant creation and recreation of the state as a moral actor and its accompanying moral responsibility in international relations.

While the variations between the different streams of constructivism are significant, they share the view that neorealism and neoliberalism pay insufficient attention to the way in which actors in international relations are socially constructed. For constructivists, power, security dilemmas, competition, and war are not inevitable features of the international system, but rather "what states make of it" (Wendt 1999, 1992).[10] From a constructivist perspective, the world is not constant, but continuously created and recreated through the social construction of knowledge and the construction of social reality. This view differs significantly from the rationalist instrumental approach to ideational factors drawn directly from microeconomics in which identities and interests are treated as exogenous and given. As explained by Adler, "social reality emerges from the attachment of meanings and functions to physical objects. Collective understandings, such as norms, endow physical objects with purpose and thus help constitute reality" (Adler 1997: 324). Such collective understandings, and their accompanying identities and interests, can become reified and embedded over time, so that alternatives seem unimaginable. It is such collective understandings that determine who actors are and how actors behave. By acting in ways that reinforce expectations of specific behavior, we are also reinforcing a social structure that exists independent of our engagement in it. This idea that we are free agents who develop our own social institutions, yet are constrained by the social structure that our free agency creates (the problem of codetermination), is the same basic philosophical conundrum that occupied Marx: people make history, but not in conditions of their own choosing.[11]

However, while this recognition of the co-constitutive relationship between agents and structures has opened up for new and innovative research in international relations in recent years, doing justice to both sides of this relationship simultaneously remains a challenge. Hence, most analyses tend to privilege either agents or structures in their explanations of events and outcomes. To avoid this difficulty, this study utilizes a relational constructivist approach, understanding both agents and structures as emerging from social networks and relations (P.T. Jackson 2006).

By challenging the dynamics of the social environment out of which both agents and structures emerge and develop, relational constructivism avoids the common tendency to treat agents as static units operating within a social context (*ibid.*; P.T. Jackson and Nexon 1999). Thus, rather than starting with an entity such as "the international community," the "UN Security Council," or the "US government" and trying to explain why it took a particular course of action when confronted with human rights violations in Rwanda, Darfur, and Libya, this study utilizes the relational constructivist approach of starting with the practical activities that continually produce and reproduce these actors and their notion of moral responsibility in international relations, and examines how these corresponding activities give rise to the observed social actions carried out in its name (Dessler 1989: 462). Particular attention is given to activities devoted to legitimation since these activities – including giving public reasons for a course of action, criticizing other options, attributing blame and responsibility, and disputing other efforts to meet set goals – are among the clearest moments at which actors are produced in practice (P.T. Jackson 2006).[12]

In the context of looking at the US government's response to situations of mass atrocities, this approach allows for the unpacking of concepts, such as what it means for "the US government" to "act." There are certain people authorized to speak on behalf of the US government in particular contexts, such as government officials and bureaucrats. When the actor speaks or acts "in the name of" the state, it is clear that they are channels or bearers of the authority of the state itself. Action, from a relational perspective, is a matter of social attribution, as certain activities are encoded or characterized as the doings of some social actor. The social attribution simultaneously produces the actor as legitimately able to perform the action in question, and legitimizes the action because this actor performs it. Legitimation processes isolate certain activities (i.e. responses to situations of severe human rights violations) and render them acceptable by characterizing them as the activities of "the state." In doing so, they reproduce the state itself. It is in these boundary demarcations that "the state" has its most tangible existence and its most concrete presence in the daily lives of those under its authority. In this view, the state is less the determinate origin of any given social action and more a product of the processes of legitimation that produce and sustain it in particular settings. Thus, the US government's authority and responsibility has to be continually negotiated and sustained in practice. Thinking of "the international community," "the UN Security Council," and "the US government" in this way allows us to grasp the stakes of the legitimation struggles – in this case, the justifications of the US government's responses to situations of severe human rights abuses – waged by politicians and other officials. An important distinction needs to be made here between politicians as individuals and politicians as representatives of "the state," because an actor such as "the state" has different rights and responsibilities, and can legitimately perform a different range of actions, than an individual actor (P.T. Jackson 2006).

Instead of evaluating statements empirically in terms of whether a specific action occurred in response to human rights atrocities (e.g., military intervention), this relational constructivist approach gives arguments a different status by viewing them instead as statements participating in an ongoing process of legitimation directed at humanitarian interventions in general and at humanitarian intervention in the cases discussed in this study in particular. In this process, statements draw on rhetorical commonplaces already present in the social environment surrounding a particular incident (Shotter 1993: 65–69; Kratochwil 1989: 40–42).[13] Specific articulations in the course of a public debate take these notions already in circulation and link them to particular policies, legitimating them and attributing them as actions to some particular actor. In this context, the question of whether "situations of genocide" or "severe human rights violations" justify "humanitarian intervention" and promote "the national interest" is considered extraneous. What matters is that these are the commonplaces invoked, and that the pairing of these commonplaces affords certain kinds of action (US intervention/leadership in intervention on behalf of the international community) while ruling others out (standing by while genocide unfolds). What makes this line of reasoning effective is precisely that it deploys existing commonplaces, so that the audience toward which the statement is directed will recognize the argument as sensible, and that it responds unequivocally to possible counter-arguments. Both of these components of a legitimation process are important aspects of this relational constructivist account (P.T. Jackson 2006).

Relational constructivism thus fulfills the mandate to preserve agency in two ways. First, rhetorical commonplaces require further specification in order to exercise their effects, and there are multiple commonplaces available in any given situation. Both the combinations of commonplaces deployed, and the specific interpretations of those commonplaces advanced by various speakers, are contingent in a way that more traditional notions of social structures are not. This contingency preserves human agency, because we cannot predict in advance what a particular speaker will do in a situation, however, whatever the speaker does do has consequential effects (*ibid.*).

The moral dimension of statecraft in US foreign policy

In the context of looking at the moral complexity of state leadership, preserving human agency is critical in order to understand the pivotal role of state leaders as norm entrepreneurs in shaping our understanding of the state as a moral actor. As pointed out by Finnemore and Sikkink (1998: 896), "norms do not appear out of thin air; they are actively built by agents having strong notions about appropriate or desirable behavior in the community." Norm entrepreneurs are critical for norm emergence and change because they form the communicative discourse involved in the presentation, deliberation, and legitimization of political ideas to the general public. Norm entrepreneurs take what is currently seen as an appropriate norm (e.g. the principle of state sovereignty and non-intervention) and re-interpret it as something that is wrong or immoral (as in cases of severe human rights violations). New norms thus commonly emerge in a highly contested normative space where they must compete with other norms and perceptions of interest. Affect, empathy, and moral beliefs may be deeply involved, since the ultimate goal is not to challenge the "truth" of something, but to challenge whether it is good, appropriate, and deserving of praise (Schmidt 2008).

Research on how moral norms influence international relations commonly focus on norm entrepreneurs operating through three channels:

• the conscience of individual national leaders;
• domestic public opinion; and
• the courtroom of world opinion (McElroy 1992).

The conscience of individual national leaders

In "Eternal Peace," Kant (in Friedrich 1949: 459) contrasts "the moral politician" with "the political moralist." The moral politician is a state leader who "employs the principles of prudence in such a way that they can coexist with morals"; while the political moralist is one "who would concoct a system of morals such as the advantage of the statesman may find convenient." Thus, while the moral politician is willing to, at times, sacrifice state interests out of a sense of moral obligation, the political moralist will manipulate moral norms to fit more narrowly defined national interests. In Kant's view, the overriding duty of the moral politician is to recognize that "the natural right of men must be held sacred, regardless of how much sacrifice is required of the powers that be" (Kant in Friedrich 1949: 469).

Yet Kant's argument, like others on the same topic, fails to adequately acknowledge the unique ethical sphere of statecraft. Due to the moral complexity of state leadership, the moral stance of policy-makers must be separated from the moral stance of individuals. R.H. Jackson (2000) refers to the ethics of statecraft as "a special ethical sphere." Acting on the ideological reservoir of the state, policy makers are at constant risk of losing moral authority by basing their decisions on precedence considerations in situations where their individual moral compass may not be compatible with state policy. Moreover, moral concerns may compete with interest-based and domestic concerns, and even with contradicting moral imperatives. To highlight the complexity of moral decision-making at the state-level, the cases in this study are contextualized historically within the presidential traditions identified by Walter Russell Mead.

Mead (2002) delineates four basic ways in which American politicians through the centuries have approached foreign policy and which influence foreign policy today. *Hamiltonians* regard a strong alliance between the national government and big business as the key to both domestic stability and effective action abroad. They focus on the nation's need to be integrated into the global economy on favorable terms. *Wilsonians* believe that the United States has both a moral obligation and an important national interest in spreading American democratic and social values throughout the world, creating a peaceful international community that accepts the rule of law. *Jeffersonians* hold that American foreign policy should be less concerned with spreading democracy abroad than with safeguarding it at home. Finally, a large populist school of *Jacksonian* foreign policy believes that the most important goal of the US government in both foreign and domestic policy should be the physical security and the economic well-being of the American people.

Drawing on these ideological traditions, state leaders are more likely to act in ways that are less congruent with their personal moral conviction than everyday individuals. By considering how these approaches impacted the responses to Rwanda, Darfur, and Libya, we can gain a more profound understanding of the complexities of moral decision-making at the state-level, revealing the contradictions inherent in the international system.

Domestic public opinion

Moreover, while states are frequently regarded as monads in international relations, internal political dynamics play a considerable role in determining external political behavior and need to be taken into consideration. Central to government decision-making processes, therefore, is the justification for why the government chooses to act in a particular way.

This experience points to a fundamental challenge in every democracy. The government needs to obtain enough legitimacy so that the forces of democratic control and domestic pressures do not prevent policy-makers from conducting a coherent, consistent, and reasonably effective long-term policy. According to Kissinger (1957: 326), "The acid test of a policy ... is its ability to obtain domestic support. This has two aspects: the problem of legitimizing a policy within the governmental apparatus ... and that of harmonizing it with the national experience." The moral premise of democracy is that those who are affected by decisions should participate in making them. The compact between leaders and citizens holds that leaders will not engage people in conflicts that threaten significant human and financial consumption unless a compelling case can be made that urgent national interests need to be protected. Yet the forces of public opinion, Congress, the media, and powerful interest groups often make themselves felt in ways that seriously complicate the ability of policy makers to pursue long-range foreign policy objectives in a coherent, consistent manner by subjecting them to constant scrutiny and evaluation. One of the characteristics of the US public is its impatience for quick results and its demand for frequent reassurances that a policy is succeeding. This impatience is often fed and exploited by the mass media and by political opponents of the administration's policy. The result of these domestic political factors is to complicate the ability of a president to pursue long-term policy with the patience and persistence that is needed. As a result, policy makers are forced to defend their long-range policy on a month-to-month or day-to-day basis. The play of public opinion and politics can distort the difficult task of evaluating the policy, erode its legitimacy, and force changes in that policy before it has had a chance to prove itself (George 2002).

Research suggests that in cases where policy-makers have offered a coherent and principled vision for intervention, public opinion has responded favorably. In situations where this type of leadership has been absent, however, public support has waned. This suggests that public opinion evaluating the practicality of humanitarian intervention, similarly to great power interests, is more accurately viewed as a dynamic force, as opposed to a static "fact," that can be shaped by visionary leadership. A policy that is consistent with fundamental values and contributes to their enhancement (normatively desirable), and feasible to execute, is considered to generate greater policy legitimacy vital to achieving a broad and stable consensus on foreign policy issues. Yet the co-constituted nature of the relationship between political leaders and the public can create formidable challenges in this regard (*ibid.*).

Correspondingly, George Kennan (1951) once made an unflattering comparison between the foreign policy of US democracy and the behavior of a dinosaur with a huge body and tiny brain: the beast is slow to rouse, but when it finally recognizes threats to its interests, it flails about indiscriminately, wrecking its native habitat while attempting to destroy its adversary. Theodore Lowi (2002) has further claimed that America's decentralized decision-making system creates incentives for leaders to adopt foreign policy threats and the "overselling" of foreign policy opportunities. Suggesting that failing US foreign policy can be attributed to excessive influence of democratic public opinion, Walter Lippmann contends:

> They [the people] have compelled the government, which usually knew what would have been wiser, or was necessary, or was more expedient, to be too late with too little, or too long with too much, too pacifist in peace and too bellicose in war, too neutralist or appeasing in negotiation or too intransigent.
>
> (Lippmann 1955: 20)

The courtroom of world opinion

This process has become even more complicated by the state's increased engagement in international affairs. International moral norms affect a state's reputation by serving as "identity indicators" that signal to the members of domestic and international society what type of state it is. However, while international moral norms can help moralize foreign policy through the pathways of conscience, domestic politics, and international reputational pressures, state decision-makers will at times find themselves in situations in which they are torn between a moral duty to follow an international moral norm and a countervailing duty to realize another and equally important moral value that conflicts with the international moral norm. Therefore, one cannot automatically assume that the policy option indicated by an international moral norm (i.e. the norm of humanitarian intervention) is the morally correct policy option. There may be instances where countervailing moral claims are of such magnitude that they outweigh the moral claim underlying the international moral norm.

Faced with the volatile tendencies of US public opinion, a president and his advisers must attempt carefully to control the public's impatience for quick results. They must also offer meaningful assurances that the cognitive premises of their policy goals and of the strategy and tactics employed on their behalf are being subjected to careful, objective evaluation. Since governments often act without knowing what the majority view is, or in contrast to what they know the majority sentiment may be, what matters more is that they have arguments that will appeal to, or at least not alienate, their own political support base, and arguments that they can use to deflate, or at least defend against, the attacks of their political opponents (Evans 2008). Moreover, the biggest constituency is most likely for inaction. Therefore, it is just as important in the international arena as it is in the domestic to be able to produce arguments appealing to morality, resource concerns, institutional interests, and political interests.

Consequently, it is not surprising that presidents at times have reacted to domestic pressures by trying to manipulate and control public opinion. While efforts to manipulate public opinion cannot be condoned, this unfortunate experience does point to a fundamental problem that every president faces; namely the problem of obtaining enough legitimacy for his policy in the eyes of Congress and public opinion so that the forces of democratic control and domestic pressures do not hobble him and prevent him from conducting a coherent, consistent, and reasonably effective long-range policy.

In principle, the criterion of "the national interest" should assist policy-makers in cutting through the complex, multi-valued nature of foreign policy issues and to improve their judgment of the relative importance of different objectives. In practice, however, the concept of the "national interest" has become so elastic and ambiguous that its role as a guide to foreign policy is highly problematic and controversial, especially when faced with situations of severe human rights violations. In the words of Arnold Wolfers (1962: 147), such "political formulas ... while appearing to offer guidance and a basis for broad consensus ... may be permitting everyone to label whatever policy he favors with an attractive and possibly deceptive name." Subsequent scholarship has illustrated the dynamics of how "the national interest" has been constructed in a variety of circumstances (Weldes 1999). It is symptomatic of the deep crisis of US foreign policy in the past decades that large elements of the public and of Congress are no longer persuaded that foreign policy actions are appropriate merely by the president's invocation of the "national interest." Skeptics have thus come to view "the national interest phrase as part of the shopworn political rhetoric that every administration in recent times has employed in order to justify questionable or arbitrary policies and decisions" (George 2002).

Situations of humanitarian intervention challenge traditional notions of what constitutes part of "national interest." Despite the recognition that there exists a responsibility to protect civilians from massacre independent of nationality, therefore, the emergence of competing moral norms on the domestic and international arena has made the question of whether situations of severe human rights violations constitute part of "national interest" one of the most controversial foreign policy issues of our time.

In response to the suggestion that situations of severe human rights violations are beyond the scope of US national interest, the US has been "nested" (Ferguson and Mansbach 1996: 50–51) within broader communities of reference such as "the West" and "humanity." Conceptually, these communities are broader than the sovereign territorial state in a number of ways: they encompass a larger geographical area, precede the sovereign territorial state historically, and in general operate at a more fundamental level than the collectivities over which national governments exercise authority. Sovereign territorial states are thus "nested" within them, almost as if the territorial borders of the state were surrounded by successive concentric circles of community membership: states belong to a civilization, which in turn belongs to humanity.

Nested community arguments are powerful rhetorical commonplaces because they function as something of a rhetorical trump card when deployed against referencing only a subordinate community, connoting as they do a concern with broader interests and values. Moreover, they justify commitments to humanitarian operations as the broader international community can make demands of its subordinate members in much the same way as "the nation" can make demands of its citizens (Anderson 1991: 9–11). Failing to go along with these demands can call a state's commitment to the larger community into question. Thus, nesting strategies engender commitment issues that can be used to combat opposition from within one's own subordinate polity, by characterizing inaction as a form of betrayal. These commitment problems only exist inasmuch as the commonplace of membership in the broader community is deployed, as the nesting strategy is the condition of possibility for the argument about displaying commitment to that superordinate community. Implicit in this discussion, therefore, lies the assumption that states operate within a system in which they are concerned with the actions of others and how such actions might affect them (a "society of states"; Bull 1977).[14]

Nested community arguments challenge pluralist notions of state morality, firmly rooted in the political reality of the current international state-system. As Morgenthau (1982: 35–36) confirms, state leaders' foremost obligation is to protect their own citizens from harm. In this view, since the international system is a world of conflict and competition in which any nation that practices altruism does so at the expense of its own citizens, altruism is an immoral act that violates the trust that their citizens put on them.

It is here, where the tension in the English School pluralist–solidarist debate finds its clearest expression. While situations of genocide or severe human rights violations bring coherence to the two theoretical positions, the policy implications of the two positions differ significantly since, "the very act of perceiving international relations in societal terms will itself condition behavior by opening new understandings of what is possible and what is desirable" (Buzan 1993: 330). Accordingly, as the following three chapters show, if we fail to acknowledge the contradictions inherent in the international system, where the responsibility of protecting citizens independent of nationality on behalf of humanity rests with state leaders elected to protect the lives and interests of their respective populations, the pledge of "never again" will most likely never become fully internalized as an actionable norm.

Notes

1 International moral skepticism is commonly associated with early theorists of the state such as Machiavelli (sometimes also referred to as a "morality of states" theorist), Bodin, and Hobbes, as well as contemporary theorists such as Morgenthau and Waltz.

2 The morality of states is represented in the work of, among others, jurists Pufendorf and Vattel, Locke, Kant (also commonly associated with cosmopolitanism), Bentham, and Mill. Contemporary "morality of states" theorists include Micahel Walzer (1994) and Benjamin Barber (2003). For elaboration on the "domestic morality analogy," see for instance Walzer (1977).

3 The natural law theories of late medieval and early modern Catholic writers such as Vitoria and Suarez, as well as the more secular international theories of Grotius, are considered cosmopolitan. Contemporary cosmopolitan scholars include Peter Singer (2009, 2004), Martha Nussbaum (2002), and Ulrich Beck (2006). Key scholars on cosmopolitan democracy include David Held (2010, 2004, 1987) and Daniele Archibugi (2009, 2003). R.B.J. Walker's (2010) efforts to deconstruct the concept of the "other," which is given context in ethics and responsibility, can also be considered cosmopolitan.

4 While solidarism and cosmopolitanism can be used interchangeably in some contexts, the distinction between the two merits clarification. From the English School perspective that international relations is a social sphere, the term "international society" covers a wide spectrum of phenomena ranging from Hobbesian social structures as "rivals" on one end, to Kantian social structures as "friends" on the other (Wendt 1999; Bull 1977). While pluralists speak for the Westphalian model, solidarists cover a spectrum from "pluralism-plus," through Kantianism, to a federation at which point the "international" dissolves into a single world polity (Buzan 2004: 140–141). It should be noted here that Bull's (1977) original formulation of solidarism was chiefly defined in terms of a consensus to enforce the law to combat the fragility of the value consensus enabling international society to operate. The purpose of Bull's argument was to warn against the international society's concomitant danger that action that undermines this consensus runs the risk of returning international relations to the more violent and conflictual condition of an international system.

5 In accommodating the fact that there is no higher authority analogous to the state in international relations, the classical writers tend to weaken the rules of restraint that states are obliged to follow, and to strengthen the principle of self-help in order to compensate for the absence of a common enforcer of law. Consequently, there is often perceived to be little difference between following the "morality of states" and the prudence of the skeptics in practice; however, Beitz (1979: 8) points out that there is an important distinction in theory, because, whereas skeptics endorse *raison d'état* because there is no higher morality, statists endorse self-help on the basis of a higher morality.

6 One could argue that also pluralist theorists' primary concern is the preser-

vation of individual rights, and that they differ from cosmopolitans simply by contending that the best way to protect individual rights is by preserving state sovereignty. For an elaboration and reframing of the pluralist–solidarist debate, see Williams (2005) and Weinert (2011), who both conceive different kinds of pluralist and solidarist positions along a spectrum.

7   It is worth clarifying here that both cosmopolitans and pluralists agree that a sense of community is an important basis for altruistic behavior, however, while pluralists consider national communities as absolute, cosmopolitans adopt a developmental framework to explain patriotism as a step on the way to cosmopolitanism.

8   Many people suspected for instance that the real motivation behind the Gulf war in the early 1990s was concern over the control of oil in the region. This suspicion accrued through a consideration of the many previous cases of aggression committed throughout the world, and against which the United States had avoided action. Examples include the reluctance of the United States to send troops to Rwanda in 1994, to Bosnia between 1992 and 1995, to Liberia in 1996, and to Sierra Leone in 1999 (Nye 2000: 152).

9   The objections to humanitarian intervention highlighted by pluralists can also be found in the writings of realists, liberals, feminists, post-colonial theorists, and others, though these different theories afford different weight to each of the objections.

10 Wendt constructs a cultural theory of international relations, consisting of "cultures of anarchy" in which whether states view each other as enemies (Hobbesian anarchy); rivals (Lockean anarchy); or friends (Kantian anarchy) is considered a fundamental determinant. Wendt's cultures of anarchy have direct parallels to Bull's (1977) Hobbesian, Grotian, and Kantian international societies.

11 In contrast to postmodernist and post-structuralist approaches, that view the world only as it can be imagined or talked about, this study draws on the methodology of thin constructivism, arguing that not all views have the same epistemic value, and that not all explanations are equally plausible (Adler 2002). Committed to a normative agenda, this study thus rejects the notion of "ideas all the way down" associated with thicker versions of constructivism.

12 The idea of reading single events through multiple interpretations and the question of legitimacy is also present in postmodernism and critical theory.

13 Rhetorical commomplaces are statements founded on an understanding commonly shared by members of an audience or community. David Bartholomae (1985: 63) defines a commonplace as "a culturally or institutionally authorized concept or statement that carries with it its own necessary elaboration … They provide points of reference and a set of 'prearticulated' explanations that are readily available to organize and interpret experience."

14 From a realist perspective, the international system maintains minimal guidelines as a baseline for acceptable state interactions, such as the principles of state sovereignty and non-intervention, and states tend to be socialized into the system as a means of survival (Waltz 1979: 127–128).

English School and constructivist scholars, on the other hand, view states as operating within an international society based on more deeply shared values and beliefs, generating greater attachment to the rules of the society (Bull 1977; Wendt 1999; Jackson 2000).

References

Adler, E. (2002) Constructivism and International Relations. In W. Carlsnaes, T. Risse, and B.A. Simmons (eds.), *Handbook of International Relations*, 112–144. London: Sage.

—— (1997). Seizing the Middle Ground: Constructivism in World Politics. *European Journal of International Relations* 3: 319–363.

Almeida, J. (2003) Pluralists, Solidarists and the Issues of Diversity, Justice and Humantarianism in World Politics. *The International Journal of Human Rights* 7(2): 144–163.

Anderson, B. (1991) *Imagined Communities: Reflections on the Origin and Spread of Nationalism*, revised edn. London: Verso.

Archibugi, D. (2009) *The Global Commmonwealth of Citizens: Toward a Cosmopolitan Democracy.* Princeton, NJ: Princeton University Press.

—— (2003) *Debating Cosmopolitics.* London: Verso.

Barber, B. (2003) *Fears Empire: War, Terrorism, and Democracy.* New York: W.W. Norton and Company.

Bartholomae, D. (1985) Inventing the University. *Journal of Basic Writing* 5(1): 4–23.

Beck, U. (2006) *Cosmopolitan Vision.* Cambridge: Polity Press.

Beitz, C. (1979) Bounded Morality: Justice and the State in World Politics. *International Organization* 33(3): 405–424.

Blair, T. (1999) Speech by UK Prime Minister Tony Blair to the Economic Club of Chicago, the Hilton Hotel, Chicago, USA, 22 April. Available at www.pbs.org/newshour/bb/international-jan-june99-blair_doctrine4-23 (accessed 13 January 2015).

Brown, C. (2009) The Only Thinkable Figure? Ethical and Normative Approaches to Refugees in International Relations. Paper presented at International Studies Association Annual Convention, New York, 15–18 February.

Bull, H. (1977) *The Anarchical Society.* New York: Columbia University Press.

Buzan, B. (2004) *From International to World Society? English School Theory and the Social Structure of Globalization.* Cambridge: Cambridge University Press.

—— (1993) From International System to International Society: Structural Realism and Regime Theory Meets the English School. *International Organization* 47(3): 327–352.

Caney, S. (1997) Human Rights and the Rights of States: Terry Nardin and Non-Intervention. *International Political Science Review* 18(1): 27–37.

Carr, E.H. (1939) *The Twenty Years Crisis: 1919–1939.* London: Macmillan.

Cochran, M. (1995) Cosmopolitanism and Communitarianism in a Post-Cold War World. In J. MacMillan and A. Linklater (eds.), *Boundaries in Question: New Directions in International Relations*. London: Pinter.

Dessler, D. (1989) What's at Stake in the Agent-Structure Debate? *International Organization* 43(3): 441–473.

Donnelly, J. (2000) *Realism and International Relations*. Cambridge: Cambridge University Press.

Dunne, T. (2008) The English School. In C. Reus-Smit and D. Snidal, (eds.), *The Oxford Handbook of International Relations*, 267–285. Oxford: Oxford University Press.

Evans, G. (2008) *The Responsibility to Protect: Ending Mass Atrocity Crimes Once and for All*. Washington, DC: Brookings Institution Press.

Ferguson, Y.H., and Mansbach, R.W. (1996) *Polities: Authority, Identities and Change*. Columbia, SC: University of South Carolina Press.

Fienberg, H. (1996) Morality Comes to IR: Ethical Approaches to the Discipline. Available at: www.hfienberg.com/irtheory/brown.html (accessed 30 July 2010).

Finnemore, M. and Sikkink, K. (1998) International Norm Dynamics and Political Change. *International Organization* 52: 887–918.

Friedrich, C.J. (1949) *The Philosophy of Kant: Immanuel Kant's Moral and Political Writings*. New York: Modern Library.

George, A. (2002) Domestic Constraints on Regime Change in US Foreign Policy: The Need for Policy Legitimacy. In J. Ikenberry (ed.), *American Foreign Policy: Theoretical Essays*, 4th edn. Boston, MA: Addison-Wesley Educational Publishers.

Held, D. (2010) *Cosmopolitanism: Ideals and Realities*. Cambridge: Polity Press.

—— (2004) *Global Covenant: The Social Democratic Alternative to the Washington Consensus*. Cambridge: Polity Press.

—— (1987) *Models of Democracy*. Cambridge: Polity Press.

Hoffman, S. (1981) *Duties Beyond Borders: On the Limits and Possibilities of Ethical International Politics*. New York: Syracuse University Press.

Jackson, P.T. (2006) Relational Constructivism: A War of Words. In J. Sterling-Folker (ed.), *Making Sense of International Relations Theory*, 139–156. London: Lynne Rienner.

Jackson, P.T. and Nexon, D. (1999) Relations Before States: Substance, Process and the Study of World Politics. *European Journal of International Relations* 5(3): 291–332.

Jackson, R.H. (2000) *The Global Covenant: Human Conduct in a World of States*. Oxford: Oxford University Press.

Kennan, G.F. (1951) *American Diplomacy 1900–1950*. Chicago, IL: University of Chicago Press.

Kissinger, H. (1957) *A World Restored: Metternich, Castlereagh and the Problems of Peace, 1812–22*. London: Phoenix Press.

Kratochwil, F. (1989) *Rules, Norms, and Decisions*. Cambridge: Cambridge University Press.

Lepard, B. (2002) *Rethinking Humanitarian Intervention: A Fresh Approach based on Fundamental Ethical Principles in International Law and World Religions.* University Park, PA: Pennsylvania State University Press.

Linklater, A. (1998) *The Transformation of Political Community: Ethical Foundations of the Post-Westphalian Era.* Cambridge: Cambridge University Press.

Lippmann, W. (1955) *Essays in the Public Philosophy.* Boston, MA: Little, Brown.

Lowi, T. (2002) *The End of Liberalism: The Second Republic and the United States*, 2nd edn. W.W. Norton and Co.

McElroy, R.W. (1992) *Morality and American Foreign Policy: The Role of Ethics in International Affairs.* Princeton, NJ: Princeton University Press.

Mead, W.R. (2002) *Special Providence.* New York: Routledge.

Morgenthau, H. (1982) *In Defense of the National Interest.* Washington, DC: University Press of America.

—— (1948) *Politics Among Nations.* New York: Alfred A. Knopf.

Nardin, T. (2008) International Ethics. In C. Reus-Smit and D.Snidal (eds.), *Oxford Handbook of International* Relations, 594–611. Oxford: Oxford University Press.

Nussbaum, M. (2002) *For Love of Country.* Boston, MA: Beacon Press.

Nye, J. (2000) *Understanding International Conflicts: An Introduction to Theory and History*, 3rd edn. New York: Addison Wesley Longman.

Ramsey, P. (2002) *The Just War: Force and Political Responsibility.* Lanham, MD: Rowman & Littlefield.

Schmidt, V.A. (2008) 'Discursive Institutionalism: The Explanatory Power of Ideas and Discourse. *Annual Review of Political Science* 11: 303–326.

Shotter, J. (1993) *Conversational Realities: Constructing Life Through Language.* London: Sage.

Singer, P. (2009) *The Life You Can Save: Acting Now to End World Poverty.* New York: Random House.

—— (2004) *One World: The Ethics of Globalization (The Terry Lectures).* New Haven, CT: Yale University Press.

Suganami, H. (2002). The International Society Perspective on World Politics Reconsidered. *International Relations of the Asia-Pacific* 2(1): 1–28.

—— (1989) *The Domestic Analogy and World Order Proposals.* Cambridge: Cambridge University Press.

Tesón, F. (2003) The Liberal Case for Humanitarian Intervention. In J.L. Holzgrefe and R.O. Keohane (eds.), *Humanitarian Intervention: Ethical, Legal, and Political Dilemmas*, 93–129. Cambridge: Cambridge University Press.

Tronto, J. (1993) *Moral Boundaries: A Political Argument for an Ethics of Care.* London: Routledge.

UN (1948) Charter of the United Nations. Available at www.un.org/en/documents/charter/index.shtml (accessed 12 January 2015).

Walker, R. (2010) *After the Globe/Before the World.* London: Routledge.

Waltz, K. (1979) *Theory of International Politics.* New York: Random House.

Walzer, M. (2000) *Just and Unjust Wars: A Moral Argument with Historical Illustrations*, 3rd edn. New York: Basic Books.

—— (1994) *Thick and Thin: Moral Argument at Home and Abroad.* Notre Dame, IN: University of Notre Dame Press.

Weinert, M.S. (2011) Reframing the Pluralist–Solidarist Debate. *Millennium – Journal of International Studies* 40: 21–41.

Weldes, J. (1999) *Constructing National Interests: the United States and the Cuban Missile Crisis.* Minneapolis, MN: University of Minnesota Press.

Wendt, A. (1999) *Social Theory of International Politics.* Cambridge: Cambridge University Press.

—— (1992) Anarchy is What States Make of It: The Social Construction of Power Politics. *International Organization* 46(3): 391–425.

Williams, J. (2005) 'Pluralism, Solidarism and the Emergence of World Society in English School Theory. *International Relations* 19(1): 19–38.

Wolfers, A. (1962) *Discord and Collaboration: Essays on International Politics.* Baltimore, MD: Johns Hopkins University Press.

2 The US response to Rwanda

> We in the United States and the world community did not do as much as we could have done to try to limit what occurred in Rwanda in 1994 … We did not act quickly enough after the killing began. We did not immediately call these crimes by their rightful name: genocide.
>
> (Clinton 1998)

During the course of 90 days following the assassination of President Juvénal Habyarimana on 6 April 1994, "Rwanda experienced the most extensive slaughter of the blood-filled" twentieth century (Clinton 1998). Armed with machetes, the Rwandan armed forces (FAR), extremist militia (Interahamwe and Impuzamugambi), and Hutu civilians engulfed the streets of Rwanda, massacring an estimated 800,000 Tutsi and moderate Hutus (OAU 1998). Despite the overwhelming evidence at the time, lack of political will bedeviled the international community, leading to inaction in response to the clearest case of genocide since the establishment of the UN Genocide Convention (UN 1951).[1]

Fifty years after the Holocaust, the international community failed again to address the heinous crime it had pledged to arrest. Concerned that the declaration of "genocide" would demand decisive action according to the UN Genocide Convention, the United States arguably led the international community in a rhetorical dance to avoid the term.

This case study suggests that the US government's dithering response to the Rwandan genocide reflected an attempt to act according to a pluralist understanding of international relations in a context challenging its limited notion of moral responsibility across political and cultural boundaries. Drawing on the ideological reservoir of the Jeffersonian foreign policy tradition, the Clinton administration justified its lack of response by referencing narrowly defined national interests, thus avoiding the pairing of commonplaces that would have warranted intervention on humanitarian grounds. This relational constructivist analysis of the Rwanda case illustrates how the deployment of certain commonplaces – and the avoidance of others – during a specific set of debates, was able to produce inaction by rendering action unacceptable to relevant audiences. Yet it also reveals how this process of legitimation simultaneously changed public expectations of how the US should respond when faced with similar situations in the future, thus shaping the identity of the state as a moral actor and how far the responsibility of this moral actor extends in international relations. Undermining the pluralist normative foundation of his own administration's practices during the 1994 "Clinton apology" by delegitimizing the beliefs on which they were based, the president advanced a solidarist expanded notion of moral responsibility by attributing moral responsibility to the US to prevent or suppress similar situations of genocide and mass atrocity in the future.

The Clinton doctrine: the struggle to promote a Jeffersonian foreign policy in an environment demanding Wilsonian engagement

The international context: opportunities and challenges

The Clinton administration entered office at a unique threshold in history, characterized by momentous opportunities and challenges. The end of the Cold War provided the new administration with an opportunity to construct a foreign policy for a new age (Haass 1997). Left standing as the world's hegemonic superpower following the termination of the defining US–Soviet rivalry, the question facing the new Clinton administration was how the United States would use its power, and for what purposes. Central to answering these questions was the identification of new threats in the new world (National Security Council Project 2000).

The collapse of the Soviet Union provided great opportunities for advancing democracy and economic prosperity. Accordingly, economic prosperity became a centerpiece of the Clinton administration's foreign policy. Clinton's 1992 slogan "Putting people first" was reflective of his Hamiltonian desire to exploit opportunities abroad for economic growth at home. Sacrificing relations with many of his supporters, Clinton passed legislation to promote free trade. In addition to the benefits

Clinton foresaw that free trade would have on the US economy through increased exports, he also believed that free trade could help move foreign nations to economic and political reform. Institutionalizing his efforts in the international realm, Clinton ratified the agreement establishing the World Trade Organization as a successor to the General Agreement on Tariffs and Trade (GATT) in 1995. This provided the organization with stronger authority to enforce trade agreements and cover a wider range of trade. With the aim of integrating domestic and international economic policy, Clinton established the National Economic Council in 1993 (National Security Council Project 2000). President Clinton's call for expansion of free markets and free governments placed questions of economic order and human freedom in the limelight.

Great challenges accompanied these opportunities. The post-Cold War era left the United States at a crossroads, lacking a coherent foreign policy (Bloch-Elkon 2007). Among the challenges that the administration identified were the proliferation of weapons of mass destruction, terrorism, and the rise of internal conflicts with potentially substantial humanitarian costs. Of particular urgency were the several crises already on the agenda during Clinton's transition into office. These crises forced the administration to engage in activities incompatible with the Jeffersonian foreign policy strategy it wished to pursue. James B. Steinberg, former deputy national security adviser and director of policy planning at the State Department, recalled:

> We had Haiti even before the administration started. You had gays in the military; you had Bosnia; and soon you had Somalia. Somalia wasn't a big problem initially, but it turned into one fairly quickly and in the first six months before you had people in place … It's an ultimate challenge when you would like to deal with the bigger, longer-term questions and do the kind of work that you do little of during the campaign … You want to do some long-term, bigger policy analysis, but the reality is that these crises take up all your time.
>
> (National Security Council Project 2000: 12)

To respond to these challenges, the Clinton administration created the first directorate dedicated to nonproliferation and export controls, as well as a directorate addressing global issues and multilateral affairs. This latter directorate was charged with the responsibility of managing challenges and opportunities in an increasingly globalized world, ranging from drug trafficking and counterterrorism to peacekeeping, humanitarian affairs, and the promotion of democracy. Yet, despite these efforts, more profound challenges hindered the Clinton administration from developing a more coherent approach to foreign policy.

Jeffersonian politics and policies: placing the "national interest" uppermost

Throughout the presidency, the Clinton administration struggled to reconcile its expressed Wilsonian intent to support the solidarist values articulated in the UN Genocide Convention with its Jeffersonian reluctance to engage in conflicts abroad rooted in fear that this might jeopardize the administration's pluralist commitment to democratic standards at home. The tension between the Wilsonian and Jeffersonian approaches to foreign policy guiding the Clinton administration was reflected in the inconsistency with which the Clinton administration put the principles of humanitarian intervention into practice and the accompanying erratic deployment of existing commonplaces to justify these responses.

Acting based on a pluralist understanding of the state as a moral actor, the Clinton administration was willing to undertake humanitarian intervention only when humanitarian motives were coupled with narrowly defined national interests. This was evident in Somalia, where the US pulled out when casualties and expenses started escalating; in Rwanda, where the lack of strategic interests led to nearly complete paralysis in response to genocide; and in Bosnia and Herzegovina, where US intervention became possible only after risks were significantly lowered by a peace agreement. Similarly, in Kosovo, while NATO members agreed to the bombing campaign of March 1999, their unwillingness to deploy ground troops prior to the formal adoption of a peace agreement demonstrated that pluralist concerns about domestic casualties outweighed the solidarist moral imperative of preventing possible genocide. Further, despite the surging rhetoric about a "new willingness" to intervene on humanitarian grounds consistently and coherently following the deployment of the Kosovo Force (KFOR) in 1999, the tension related to how far moral responsibility extends in international relations was reflected in the gap between discourse and action. This gap was widened by the subsequent lack of response to significant human rights violations in other parts of the world, such as Sierra Leone, the Democratic Republic of the Congo, and Chechnya.

A memorandum for the vice president and others, Presidential Decision Directive (PDD) 25, titled US Policy on Reforming

Multilateral Peace Operations (White House 1994a), and its accompanying press release (White House 1994b), highlight the Clinton administration's pluralist policies and priorities, placing "our national interest uppermost." Developed against the backdrop of the Somalia meltdown (discussed below), this directive became the doctrinal lynchpin for the Clinton administration's policy of reluctance in response to conflicts in Africa. Contextualizing US support for multilateral peace operations within an environment of "serious threats to the security of the United States," the Clinton administration "remains committed to meeting such threats through either unilateral or multilateral action, as our interests dictate" (White House 1994a). However, according to the press release, multilateral operations must "be placed in proper perspective among the instruments of US foreign policy" (White House 1994b). Reflecting a limited pluralist understanding of the US as a moral actor in international relations, the PDD 25 emphasizes that any UN operation must "advance US interests," while also limiting US participation in UN missions, as well as US support for other states that intend to carry out UN-sanctioned missions (White House 1994a). This instrumental approach to multilateralism is further reflected in the statement that the UN can serve as "an important instrument" in situations where "it will be in our interest to proceed in partnership with others," and as a "force multiplier" in US "efforts to promote peace and stability" (*ibid.*). While reiterating that "UN peace operations can never substitute for the necessity of fighting and winning our own wars," it suggests that "since it is in our interest to support or participate in UN peace operations on such occasions, it is also in our interest to seek to strengthen our own and the United Nations' peace operations capabilities" (*ibid.*).

The limited "national interest" argument for support of multilateral peace operations is further reflected in PDD 25's press release (White House 1994b), which invokes the term "national interest" 25 times while referring to "collective interests" once. The press release reasons: "the establishment of a capability to conduct multilateral peace operations is part of our National Security Strategy and National Military Strategy" (*ibid.*). It contends that US participation can "be necessary to persuade others to participate in operations that serve US interests," and can "enable the US to exercise influence "without unilaterally bearing the burden" and because the US may "be called upon and choose to provide unique capabilities to important operations that other countries cannot" (*ibid.*). Accordingly, "It is important to build public and Congressional support for UN peace operations, particularly those in which US forces participate" (White House 1994a). Though not officially implemented until 4 May, the PDD 25 directive was used as an informal guide for US policy toward Rwanda, augmented by a general indifference regarding Rwandan affairs.

Thus, contrary to the widely held perception that the Clinton administration pursued a Wilsonian foreign policy, the government was characterized by a Jeffersonian reluctance to engage in conflicts abroad – combined with an Hamiltonian desire to pursue favorable economic relations internationally – but was forced to address the international political environment in which it operated, leading to inconsistency in policy. Initially viewed as an actor primarily responsible for the protection and promotion of narrowly defined national interests, the political climate during the Clinton administration challenged this pluralist limited notion of the state as a moral actor. This left the Clinton administration with the difficult task of shaping practice and discourse to fit this new climate, and to address its accompanying conflicting pluralist–solidarist expectations. Clinton failed to clearly articulate a foreign policy that could justify its inconsistent responses to situations of severe human rights violations. By invoking rhetorical commonplaces capriciously, the statements deployed were not recognized as sensible by the audiences toward which they were directed. A brief look at the Somalia case further exposes the highly contested normative space contextualizing the US response to Rwanda.

The legacy of Somalia

While not treated as a separate case study in itself, the collapse of the UN mission in Somalia deserves brief consideration as crucial to understanding the US response to Rwanda. Just weeks before Clinton took office, President George H. W. Bush had deployed American soldiers to Somalia, where people were suffering from civil war and starvation. The soldiers were sent to guard food and other relief supplies from being stolen by warring factions (White House 1993). However, when the US publicly named Mohamad Farrah Aidid as enemy number one – following the catastrophic firefight that left 24 Pakistani UN soldiers dead, and the passing of UN resolution 837, ordering the arrest of those responsible for the massacre – US troops were effectively transformed from humanitarian agents to combatants in a local conflict abroad.

On 3 October 1993, two US Black Hawk helicopters were shot down and three others were damaged in a battle against Somali militia fighters loyal to Aidid. As part of the UN mission, 18 American soldiers were killed and 84 were wounded (Frontline 1998). Images broadcasting

American soldiers being dragged through the streets of Mogadishu generated loud protests, challenging the president's ability to justify the intervention by referencing US "national interests." Motivated by a solidarist commitment to prevent further anarchy and accompanying starvation for Somalia's civilians, and in an attempt to assist US Forces in defending themselves, President Clinton initially increased US presence in Somalia.

However, failing to justify the sacrifice of American lives in defense of Somali civilians, demands for withdrawal grew louder, forcing Clinton to withdraw all US troops in March 1994, leaving Somalia in a state of anarchy with warlords battling for control (Military.com 2009). The public's response to the intervention in Somalia reveals how affect, empathy, and moral beliefs shape what is considered good, appropriate, and deserving of praise in situations where new norms emerge to compete with other norms and perceptions of interest. While initial support for intervention was strong, the brutal images of American soldiers being dragged through the streets in Mogadishu served to reinforce the boundaries between "Americans" and "foreigners" and the sense that the US government's primary responsibility as a moral actor should remain the protection of American lives and interests. The pairing of rhetorical commonplaces such as "situations of genocide" or "severe human rights violations," with "humanitarian intervention" and "the national interest" did not generate adequate support to advance a solidarist understanding of the state as a moral actor.

The Somalia intervention dramatically altered the United States' commitment to peacekeeping, especially in Africa. While initially a demonstration of the Clinton administration's solidarist commitment to the Genocide Convention and the Universal Declaration of Human Rights, the lack of "proper" effectuation of this solidarist commitment engendered significant problems. The Clinton administration was severely criticized for their intervention in what was later referred to as the "Somalia disaster," causing hesitation with regard to placing troops in a similar situation in Rwanda.

Beyond Somalia, the US had four additional major peacekeeping operations in Africa at the time when the genocide in Rwanda unfolded. There were concerns at the National Security Council, the State Department, and the Defense Department about expanding this long list of peacekeeping operations in Africa alone. The press statement on the reformation of multilateral peace operations (discussed above) relates the Clinton administration's Jeffersonian attempt at meeting this challenge:

It is not US policy to seek to expand either the number of UN peace operations or US involvement in such operations. Instead, this policy, which builds upon work begun by previous administrations and is informed by the concerns of the Congress and our experience in recent peace operations, aims to ensure that our use of peace-keeping is selective and more effective.

(White House 1994b)

This hesitation to develop a long-term policy for consistent responses to severe human rights violations reflects the Clinton administration's struggle to reconcile its recognized solidarist commitment to international agreements with a continued commitment to the state as a pluralist moral actor.

Domestic contradictions

Beyond the challenge of pursuing a Jeffersonian foreign policy guided by a pluralist limited understanding of moral responsibility in an international environment ripe with situations of severe human rights violations and mounting pressure on the permanent members of the UN Security Council to respond, President Clinton quickly found himself to be the head of an administration attempting to execute a foreign policy with little support from Pentagon or the Congress. In foreign policy, the federal government has significant power with minimal if any power reserved to the individual states. Within the federal government, power to influence public opinion is concentrated most notably in the executive branch. Yet experience suggests that American presidents more commonly follow, as opposed to lead, public opinion. Domestic political advisers play a prominent and often decisive role in major foreign policy decision-making processes. During the Clinton administration, Jeffersonians and Jacksonians dominated the Pentagon and Congress, promoting a foreign policy based on pluralist, narrowly defined national interests and minimum engagement in humanitarian situations abroad. The pressure away from international engagement was exacerbated when insurgent Republicans, many with strong Jacksonian leanings, took control of Congress in 1994 (Mead 2002). In an effort to rally Congressional support for peace operations, the PDD 25 press release states the importance of Congress being actively involved in the implementation of US policy on peacekeeping:

To sustain US support for UN peace operations, Congress and the American people must understand and accept the potential value of such operations as tools of US interests. Congress and the American people must also be genuine participants in the processes that support US decision-making on new and on-going peace operations. Traditionally, the Executive branch has not solicited the involvement of Congress or the American people on matters related to UN peacekeeping. This lack of communication is not desirable in an era when peace operations have become more numerous, complex and expensive. The Clinton Administration is committed to working with Congress to improve and regularize communication and consultation on these important issues.

(White House 1994b)

The Clinton administration thus found itself in a complex and challenging position. As the case of Rwanda reveals, the administration's Hamiltonian and Jeffersonian efforts to remain focused on the promotion of pluralist, narrowly defined national economic and security interests, was incompatible with the challenges of the time, demanding international engagement based on a solidarist expanded notion of moral responsibility. Questions related to why the US was obliged to be involved in or support these missions framed the context within which the genocide in Rwanda emerged on the international agenda.

Rwanda

When I came out, there were no birds. There was sunshine and the stench of death.

(Rwandan genocide survivor, cited in
Human Rights Watch 1999: n.p.)

The genocide in Rwanda created an unprecedented opportunity for the United States to provide political and moral leadership in the development of a blueprint for post-Cold War collective security responses to mass atrocities. In contrast to the slow damage occurring in Bosnia and Herzegovina at the time, the velocity of the Rwandan genocide commanded the attention of the international community. As explained by Ronayne (2001: 152), the brutal events in central Africa put the UN Convention on the Prevention and Punishment of the Crime of Genocide and "the hegemonic influence of the United States to the test;

Rwanda dared the outside world to act against a heinous international crime it had pledged to arrest."

However, rather than seizing the opportunity to invigorate the ethical vision embedded in the text of the UN Genocide Convention, the United States hesitated. As information about Rwanda's unfolding genocide became increasingly available, the Clinton administration sought, as in Bosnia, to avoid, minimize, and redefine genocide in progress to eschew discourse not compatible with the pluralist limited notion of moral responsibility guiding the Jeffersonian Clinton administration. Secretary of State Warren Christopher did not authorize officials to use the term "genocide" until 21 May, and even then, US officials waited another three weeks before using the term in public. Beyond the discursive efforts to undermine the situation in Rwanda in order to avoid expectations warranting undesirable action – and contrary to later public statements – the US lobbied the UN for a total withdrawal of UN forces in Rwanda in April 1994. Domestic politics, dominated by democratic infighting; the legacy of Somalia; and narrowly defined national interests produced consistent delays and impediments as hundreds of thousands were massacred under the Hutu extremists' genocidal assault.

Challenging the dynamics of the social environment within which the US government's response to the Rwandan genocide emerged, this relational constructivist case reveals an actor constructed by a limited pluralist understanding of moral responsibility in international relations, challenged by a demand for increased solidarist engagement. By evaluating the practical measures and moral justifications of the US government in response to the genocide in Rwanda, it unpacks how the pairing of commonplaces reflective of a limited notion of moral responsibility served to justify inaction during the genocide. However, it also reveals an administration torn between its pluralist and solidarist commitments. The case demonstrates how the recognition of its solidarist obligations simultaneously contributed to inaction in response to Rwanda, and to the advancement of an expanded solidarist notion of moral responsibility in international relations by later acknowledging its failure to meet its commitment to the 1948 UN Genocide Convention. Thus, the US response to Rwanda served to strengthen the expectation that the pairing of concepts such as "genocide" with "national interests" affords certain kinds of action (i.e. humanitarian intervention) while ruling out the possibility of standing by while genocide unfolds.

Background: the Arusha Accords and increasing instability

The tension between Hutus and Tutsis has a long history. The two main ethnic groups have struggled for power since the country was awarded to Belgium by the League of Nations after the First World War. The Belgians had groomed the Tutsis as a ruling class to enforce colonial order against the Hutus, however, this order was reversed by the time Rwanda gained independence in 1962. Following a successful coup by Hutu leader Juvénal Habyarimana in 1973, Rwanda entered a period of relative peace and stability. By the 1990s, however, the country faced serious economic problems as coffee prices fell on the world market and poor weather conditions contributed to food shortages. The combination of internal economic disruptions and external enemies provided fertile ground for tension and violence. Reinvigorating massacre as a political tool, militia forces and Hutu militants attacked and killed hundreds of Tutsi in separate incidents from late 1990 to 1993 (Lebor 2006). Yet, even in a country with a history as turbulent as that of Rwanda, the scale and speed of the atrocities yet to occur went far beyond the imaginable.

The growing violence and dangerous instability did not go unnoticed. Aware of the tensions in Rwanda, the international community facilitated the negotiation of the end of the civil war between the president of Rwanda and the Rwandan Patriotic Front (RPF). Under the auspices of the Organization of African Unity (OAU), Tanzania mediated the negotiations. To provide additional sources of leverage, representatives from France, Germany, the US, and the UN attended the talks as observers. Similarly, Burundi, Uganda, Zaire, and the OAU sent observers to demonstrate regional anxiety about the settlement (Incore 1993).

The Arusha Accords, signed on 4 August 1993, established a system of power sharing and political reform, promoting multiethnic democracy, and the fundamental freedom and rights of individuals in Rwanda. A transitional government included representatives from the Rwandan Patriotic Front. The UN Assistance Mission for Rwanda (UNAMIR) was charged with overseeing the implementation of the accords and military observers from the Organization of African Unity monitored the cease-fire. The initial UNAMIR force was composed of 800 soldiers with a total of 2,500 envisioned for final deployment. From the outset, however, the implementation of the Arusha Accords confronted several obstacles.

Most importantly, while President Habyarimana did open the government to Tutsi representatives and appointed a moderate opposition party Hutu, Agathe Uwilingiyimana, as prime minister, he "had no principled commitment to the accords and temporized on their implementation at every step" (Burkhalter 1994–1995: 44). Instead, Habyarimana was a believer in "Hutu power" ideology – Hutu superiority, Hutu rule and domination, and the need to deal harshly with the supposedly subversive Tutsi minority (Lebor 2006). The Arusha Accords ended President Habyarimana's 20-year one-party rule over Rwandan politics and society. As the accords were being negotiated, Habyarimana's supporters and their militias intensified their efforts to defeat the implementation of the agreement.

Critical to mobilizing popular support among ordinary Hutus was the radio station Radio Télévision Libre Mille Collines (RTLMC). Evoking the historical domination of Tutsis and the fear of an armed Tutsi insurrection to mobilize support, RTLMC broadcasts accused the Tutsis of being plotters and parasites. Advising its listeners to identify Tutsis by examining their physical appearance – to "look at their small noses, and then break them" – RTLMC called on listeners to take action against the "infiltrators" and their "cockroach" accomplices. After 6 April 1994, RTLMC broadcast increasingly more virulent calls for violence and explicitly urged its listeners to exterminate the Tutsi from the surface of the earth so that future generations would only be able to guess what Tutsis looked like, insisting, "We have to act ... wipe them all out." According to General Romeo Dallaire, "RTLMC was created specifically as a tool of the genocidaires to demonize the Tutsi, lay the ground work, then literally drive on the killing once the genocide started" (Otiti 2010).

Only one week after the accords were signed, the United Nations published a report, warning of serious risk of genocide in Rwanda. The report stated, "The victims of the attacks, Tutsis in the overwhelming majority of cases, have been targeted solely because of their membership of a certain ethnic group and for no other objective reason" (UN Economic and Social Council 1993: 22).

Failing to understand the dynamics within Rwanda, and the intentions of the Hutu extremists groups, many assumed that the Arusha peace process would stabilize the country. The peace process was believed to provide the foundation for the development of a UN presence and the means to support what was understood to be a genuine government commitment to the peace process. While Kagame, the military commander of the RPF, raised concerns about the participation of extremist Hutu groups in the transitional government, the international community accommodated Habyarimana's insistence on their inclusion. Romeo Dallaire, the Force Commander of the United Nations Assistance Mission for Rwanda (UNAMIR) was furious, recognizing that the UN was falling into a trap. George Moose, former US Assistant Secretary of State for African Affairs, recalls:

> I have to say when I left my meeting with Kagame in Kampala, I was having some of the same doubts [as Dallaire]. I mean, he made a very forceful case as to why [the extremist Hutus] should not be allowed in any government, and it was hard frankly to disagree with him. [But] I don't know if other things hadn't intervened when I got back to Washington [that I] would have raised this question and said, "We need to revisit this."
>
> (Frontline 2004)

Despite these concerns, failing to identify alternative approaches to deal with the situation in Rwanda, speculations about the ingenuity of President Habyarimana were ignored in favor of the peace process. The fragility of the situation was later revealed not only to undermine the entire premise of the agreement, but also to facilitate the genocide that followed.

By agreeing to the Arusha Accords, Habyarimana literally signed his own "death warrant" (Keane 1995: 27). In addition to the sacrifices involved in giving up power to the Tutsis, the Hutu extremists were further emboldened by the assassination of the Burundian democrati- cally elected Hutu President Melchior Ndadaye by the Tutsi army. This resulted in the influx of approximately 200,000 Hutu refugees into Rwanda who were ripe for political mobilization in areas of the country where the architects of mass extermination feared most resistance to their policies. This unstable regional environment compounded the Agreement's internal fragility, further debilitating the implementation process.

Moreover, both the mediators and parties to the Arusha Agreement staked its implementation almost exclusively on international actors who were unwilling and ill prepared to expend resources on meeting most of its provisions. For the international community, deployment was contingent on discernible movement toward peace and the estab- lishment of transitional institutions. A memorandum to the Under Secretary of Defense for Policy, titled Talking Points on Rwanda/Burundi, states the US policy of not being willing to get involved "until peace is restored":

> As the only 'honest broker' left on the field (given the intense hatred of Belgium by the Rwandan Hutus and of France by the

Tutsis) we could (and should) play a critical diplomatic role in urging the parties to adhere to the Arusha peace agreement. We would want to restart our security assistance program once the peace process is back on track [parentheses in the original].

(US Department of State 1994a)

For the parties to the conflict, however, there would be limited progress in key provisions without full UNAMIR deployment. A day before the genocide began, the Security Council met to discuss whether UNAMIR's mandate to monitor the ceasefire and oversee the implementation of the accords, established in Resolution 872, should be renewed for another six months. Under pressure from the US and the UK it was agreed in Resolution 909 that the UN would pull out in six weeks unless the transitional government was created. From the outset, conflicting goals about deployment and intervention had marked the UNAMIR enterprise. The underfunded UN force, mandated only to monitor the ceasefire, sent a powerful signal to the extremists that they could act with impunity. Incidentally, Rwanda was a member of the Security Council at this time and hence its Ambassador was well aware of the reluctance of the US to stop the continuation of UNAMIR.

Among the strongest opponents to reinforcing the peacekeepers in Rwanda and providing a stronger mandate to intervene to halt the bloodshed was the UK Ambassador to the UN Security Council, Sir David Hannay. Hannay suggested that intervention would lead to a repetition of Somalia where, seven months earlier, the Council had suffered a humiliating defeat when the UN peace mission had spiraled out of control. The US and others echoed these concerns (US House Foreign Affairs Committee 1994). Despite the moral groundswell of support for action among the advocacy community caused by the prospect of genocide, there was widespread apprehension among members of the Security Council. The major concern was that were the UN to suffer another disaster like Somalia with more peacekeepers being killed, the UN would suffer a possibly fatal blow to its credibility (Barnett 1997). The extreme unlikelihood of a ceasefire meant that any potential UN intervention force would be thrust into a civil war. Hannay reminded the members of the Security Council to "think back to Somalia and think about what you would ask these troops to do." He suggested that the UN peacekeepers be withdrawn, and that a "token force" remain behind in Rwanda to "appease public opinion" (Williams's interview with Sir David Hannay, Birmingham, 12 March 2003, cited in Melvern and Williams 2004).

This sentiment reflected the pluralist notion of moral responsibility guiding the members of the UN Security Council during their deliberations. The Secretariat and Security Council had a moral responsibility to protect the UNAMIR soldiers. This had to be weighed against the protection they were providing for Tutsis and moderate Hutus. According to a classified cable from the US Department of State to the US Mission to the United Nations (US Department of State 1994b), "to attempt to sustain a peacekeeping operation in the present environment would only undermine the Security Council's responsibilities for international peacekeeping." On 21 April, the UN Security Council passed Resolution 912 to withdraw the peacekeepers, leaving a token 270. UNAMIR's withdrawal two weeks after the genocide was instigated, gave the extremists an opportunity to wage the genocide for two more months. Although Boutros-Ghali rightly described the withdrawal as a "scandal," this decision simply ended an outrageous phase that had started with unrealistic expectations enshrined in the Arusha agreement (Khadiagala 2001).

Early warnings and response: the United Nations

Warnings of an impending genocide were countless and clear. At the end of August 1993, amid escalating levels of violence, Prime Minister Uwilingiyimana warned that growing insecurity did not "augur well for the implementation of the [Arusha] Agreement because security is a prerequisite for successful implementation" (cited in Khadiagala 2001: 12). In December 1993, UN peacekeepers received an anonymous letter from Hutu army officers warning of a plan for assassinations and massacres. On 11 January 1994, UNAMIR commander General Romeo Dallaire reported urgently to the UN Peacekeeping Office information he had received about weapons stockpiles, government and militia plans to exterminate Tutsis, and plans to kill Belgian soldiers "and thus guarantee Belgian withdrawal from Rwanda." The details came to Dallaire from an informant working with Hutu militias and government officials. It continued, "he [the informant] has been ordered to register all Tutsi in Kigali. He suspects it is for their extermination. Example he gave was that in 20 minutes his personnel could kill up to 1000 Tutsis." Urging action, Dallaire closed the later infamous "genocide fax" with these words: *"Peux ce que veux. Allons-y"* ("Where there's a will, there's a way. Let's go").

The reply from the UN Peacekeeping Office, headed by Kofi Annan, was immediate. The cable from Iqbal Riza (Annan 1994), who was handling Rwanda for Annan, to Jacques-Roger Booh Booh, the head of UNAMIR read, "Information is cause for concern but there are certain inconsistencies. We must handle this information with caution." Annan and Riza instructed Dallaire not to take action but to share the information with the Belgians, French, and American missions and with the Habyarimana government. Riza (Frontline 2004) recalls, "We said, not Somalia again." Due to these concerns, Dallaire's fax never reached the Security Council. David Hannay, British Permanent Representative to the United Nations Security Council, remembers, "None of us [in the Security Council] saw Dallaire's fax, as the Secretariat never passed the information along."

The concerns with regard to the distribution of arms, the activities of the militia, killings, and increased ethnic tension continued throughout the early months of 1994. In a cable to Annan and Under-Secretary General for Political Affairs, James Jonah, on 2 February, Booh Booh wrote that the security situation was deteriorating on a daily basis and that the peacekeeping operation would be in jeopardy without prompt confiscation of arms stockpiled by the militia. He predicted "more frequent and more violent demonstrations, more grenade and armed attacks on ethnic and political groups, more assassinations and quite possibly outright attacks on UNAMIR installations" (UN Security Council 1999).

Following these predictions of impending violence, Belgian Foreign Minister Willy Claes approached the Security Council for an extended mandate for the UN forces in Rwanda. Claes asked the Council for more authority to act to strengthen the Belgian-led force and allow it to seize weapons caches. In a letter to the Secretary-General on 14 March 1994, Claes echoed General Dallaire's concerns:

> Current political developments in the situation in Rwanda are not encouraging ... As you are aware, the deadlock in the formation of a broad-based transitional government is leading, despite the efforts of your Special Representative, to a deterioration of the political climate. The Rwandese army appears increasingly annoyed by the parties' procrastination, while information on the stockpiling of weapons by the various militias is becoming even more compelling. Even some of the leaders admit that a prolongation of the current political deadlock could result in an irreversible explosion of violence ... It seems to me, however, that [the] higher profile of the United Nations on the political level should be accompanied by a firmer stance on the part of UNAMIR with

respect to security ... Unless the negative developments we are witnessing are halted, UNAMIR might find itself unable to continue effectively its basic mission of playing a major supporting role in the implementation of the Arusha Peace Agreement.

(Claes 1994)

Desiring no additional risk for UNAMIR, however, a declassified cable from Belgium's UN delegation to Brussels reports that the US vetoed Belgium's request to augment its own forces on the ground (Hentoff 1999: 28). Consequently, on 7 April 1994, when the Rwandan presidential guard captured and assassinated Prime Minister Agathe Uwilingiyimana, her husband, as well as the ten Belgian soldiers assigned to protect them, Claes's warning materialized. This dramatic episode drove Belgium into a depressive consternation which entailed Belgium's disengagement from UNAMIR. As to justify its decision, Belgium carried the UN along with a spiraling number of countries who were leaving UNAMIR, leaving only a skeletal peacekeeping force. This incident exposed the question of whether a moral responsibility to protect others involves a corresponding duty to sacrifice the self in doing so – which was answered in the negative. The international community thus confirmed the assumption of the people behind the genocide, who were counting on the fact that western nations could not tolerate their own casualties without pulling out the mission.

Following this incident, Secretary of State Warren Christopher instructed Madeleine Albright, America's Ambassador at the UN, to push for removing the entire peacekeeping force (US Department of State 1994b). The official US line was that the killings in Rwanda were not genocide, but part of the resumption of hostilities in the civil war. This precludes, by definition, the use of peacekeepers (Lewis 1994). Advising that the withdrawal did not require a UN Security Council resolution, which would most likely have attracted international criticism, the Department instructed the mission "that we will oppose any effort at this time to preserve a UNAMIR presence in Rwanda." The telegram reads: "the Department believes that there is insufficient justification to retain a UN peacekeeping presence in Rwanda and that the international community must give highest priority to full, orderly withdrawal of all UNAMIR personnel as soon as possible." The pluralist limited moral principle highlighted by Vetlesen (2000: 530) in the case of Bosnia that "The execution of the mandate ... is secondary to the security of UN personnel" was reflected in the UN order: "USUN is instructed to inform NSC [National Security Council] colleagues that the United States believes that the first priority of the Security Council is to instruct the Secretary General to implement an orderly withdrawal of all/all UNAMIR forces from Rwanda …"

The practical and discursive response to Rwanda reveals the government's struggle to reconcile its pluralist and solidarist commitments. Despite President Clinton's clearly articulated intent to act according to a pluralist limited understanding of moral responsibility in international relations, the United States' failure to uphold its solidarist commitment to the Genocide Convention, troubled US officials. Albright (Frontline 2004) recalls, "My instructions were to support full withdrawal. I listened to the discussions very carefully in the Security Council. I could see that our position was wrong … I had these instructions which made no sense at all." Albright left the informal meetings of the Security Council to call Washington. Rather than calling the State Department that had issued the instructions, she called the National Security Council, which was dealing with Rwanda on an imminent basis, in the hope that she would get a better hearing. She spoke with Richard Clarke who was in charge of peacekeeping. Clarke said, "Well, no, we're worrying about this, and these are your instructions. I actually screamed into the phone. I said, they are unacceptable. I want them changed" (*ibid.*). Despite Albright's attempts, the UN Security Council, at the behest of the United States, which had no troops in Rwanda, voted to withdraw all but a remnant of UNAMIR on 21 April 1994. While this conversation was taking place at the UN, the interim Council of Ministers in Rwanda, aware that the UN Security Council was in retreat, decided to expand their extermination program from Kigali to the rest of the country. "It was an almost surreal issue," records Colin Keating, president of the Security Council in April 1994: "While thousands of human beings were being slaughtered every day, ambassadors argued fitfully in New York for weeks about military tactics" (Keating 2004: 509).

After human rights, media, and diplomatic reports of the carnage mounted, the UN finally decided to deploy UNAMIR II, a more robust force of 5,500 troops on 16 May 1994. However, delayed by prolonged discussions about the financial and practical aspects of the deployment of these troops, the full complement of troops and material would not arrive in Rwanda until months after the genocide ended. The most successful contribution of the international community toward ending the atrocities in Rwanda was its support of the French intervention on 22 June. Frustrated by the UN's delay and concerned about its image as a former patron and arms supplier to the Habyarimana government, France announced on 15 June that they would intervene to stop the killing. The UN Security Council approved this intervention on 22 June and French troops immediately entered Rwanda from Zaire. However, confronted by the RPF's rapid advance across Rwanda, the French set up a "humanitarian zone" in the southwest corner of Rwanda. The French intervention succeeded in saving tens of thousands of Tutsi lives. However, it also facilitated the safe exit of many of its allies responsible for the planning and execution of the genocide (Ferroggiaro 2001).

The reluctant response of the UN to the warnings of impending violence in Rwanda reflects the tension inherent in the UN system. While established to protect and promote humanity's interests, the UN relies on its members to carry out its mandate. As the Rwandan genocide so clearly demonstrates, in situations where "humanity's interests" are not considered compatible with "national interests" as defined by its members capable of carrying out a UN mandate, the international community runs the risk of complete paralysis. An in-depth relational constructivist analysis of the United States' practical and discursive response to Rwanda further reveals the dilemmas associated with the crucial role of the "Big Five" – and particularly the United States as its strongest member in the post-Cold War era – to the development of more coherent and consistent responses to situations of severe human rights violations.

Early warnings and the United States' practical response

Hello, this is Prudence Bushnell. Stop it. Stop killing people.
(US Deputy Assistant Secretary for African Affairs Prudence
Bushnell, in Frontline 2004)

Owing to the declassification of numerous US State Department memos, Central Intelligence Agency briefings, and other sensitive government materials, it is now well documented that the United States had considerable knowledge of what was happening to Rwandan Tutsis and moderate Hutus in April through June 1994. At the end of January 1994, the CIA conducted a study suggesting that potential combat in Rwanda would include violence against civilians with a worst-case scenario of the deaths of half a million people. Similarly, in a meeting between American and Rwandan public officials in March 1994, the US Deputy Assistant Secretary for African Affairs, Prudence Bushnell, told Habyarimana that Rwanda was "in an historic transition, one which historians would record as being glorious, or ignominious and tragic"

(US Embassy in Kigali 1994). The US officials registered "deep concern over the mounting violence in Rwanda," as well as "the distribution of arms and arms caches."

On 10 April, the *New York Times* (McFadden 1994) quoted the International Red Cross claim that "tens of thousands" were dead and that corpses were "in the houses, in the streets, everywhere." The same day, the *Washington Post* (Richburg 1994) described "a pile of corpses six feet high" outside the main hospital. On 16 April, the *New York Times* reported the slaughter of nearly 1,200 men, women, and children in the church where they had sought refuge. On 19 April, Human Rights Watch estimated the number of dead at 100,000 and called for use of the term "genocide." On 24 April, the *Washington Post* reported how "the heads and limbs of victims were sorted and piled neatly, a bone-chilling order in the midst of chaos that harked back to the Holocaust" (Parmalee 1994). On 9 May, a Defense Intelligence Agency report observed that the Rwandan violence was not spontaneous, but systematically directed by the government toward a list of prominent Tutsi and moderate Hutu sympathetic to reconciliation:

> Multiple sources indicate that the violence by the Presidential Guard and various youth militias was not spontaneous, but was directed by high-level officials within the interim government. It appears that, in addition to the random massacres ... there is an organized, parallel effort of genocide being implemented by the army to destroy the leadership of the Tutsi community. The original intent was to kill only the political elite supporting reconciliation; however, the government lost control of the militias, and the massacre spread like wildfire.
>
> (US Defense Intelligence Agency 1994)

On the ground in Rwanda, Joyce Leader, second-in-command at the US Embassy in Kigali (Frontline 2004) recalls, "The people tried to tell us [the US Embassy] and tried to explain to us or help us understand, but we just, maybe we just didn't get it. It was just very hard to conceive of something so awful actually being meticulously planned and carried out."

These many warnings of ethnic violence on a large scale in Rwanda caused little concern in the US. On the contrary, the Deputy Assistant Secretary for African Affairs, James Woods was asked to remove Rwanda and Burundi from the list of potential crisis areas generated after the Clinton administration took office because involvement in these conflicts was not considered to promote "US national interest":

I won't go into personalities, but I received guidance from higher authorities: "Look if something happens in Rwanda-Burundi, we don't care. Take it off the list. US national interest is not involved and we can't put all these silly humanitarian issues on lists like important problems like the Middle East, North Korea, and so on. Just make it go away."

(Frontline 2004)

Not surprisingly, Rwanda did not go away. The plane crash on 6 April 1994, killing Rwandan President Juvénal Habyarimana and his Burundian counterpart Cyprien Ntaryamira, sparked the violence that over 90 days cost the lives of an estimated 800,000 Rwandans. Within an hour of the plane crash, the Presidential Guard, elements of the Rwandan armed forces (FAR) and extremist militia (Interahamwe and Impuzamugambi) set up roadblocks and barricades and began the organized slaughter, starting in the capital Kigali. Their first targets were those most likely to resist the plan of genocide: the opposition Prime Minister, the president of the constitutional court, priests, leaders of the Liberal Party and Social Democratic Party, the Information Minister, and tellingly, the negotiator of the Arusha Accord (Ferroggiaro 2001).

Motivated by a pluralist understanding of the US government as a moral actor and the accompanying limited notion of moral responsibility in international relations, US State representatives were primarily concerned with the effects of these upheavals on US citizens in Rwanda. A memorandum from Prudence Bushnell (US Department of State 1994c) to Secretary of State Christopher read, "Both our Embassies … have instructed the American community to stay at home until further notice. All Americans are believed safe. There are no Peace Corps volunteers in either country." Yet, despite this seemingly calm assessment, a memorandum to the Under Secretary of Defense for Policy, "Talking Points on Rwanda/Burundi" (US Department of State 1994a) reveals the Pentagon's candid estimation only five days after the president's plane had been shot down that "unless both sides can be convinced to return to the peace process, a massive (hundreds of thousands of deaths) bloodbath will ensue that would likely spill over into Burundi." The analysts concluded that "civilians will increasingly be drawn into the conflict," and that "it is highly likely that inter-tribal killings will spread" to Burundi. "In addition, millions of refugees will flee into neighboring Uganda, Tanzania, and Zaire, far exceeding the absorptive capacity of those nations" (*ibid.*).

From a pluralist perspective that the primary responsibility of a state leader is the protection of its own citizens, it is not surprising that the lack of national interest involved in Rwanda generated the response of the United States and other Western states to evacuate their nationals from embassies and diplomatic missions. Reflecting the sentiment at the time, the US Secretary of State, Warren Christopher, commented that evacuating US nationals was "the prudent thing to do." This pluralist moral approach reflected the general sentiment of a distinction between nationals and foreigners, even a sentiment of apathy against the Rwandese, echoed by influential members of Congress such as Robert Dole (R-KS), who remarked, "the Americans are out, and as far as I'm concerned, in Rwanda, that ought to be the end of it" (CBS 1994).

Commonly considered the penultimate US initiative during the genocide, a White House press statement on 22 April 1994 (White House 1994b) called on four Rwandan military leaders to "end the violence." Urged by Human Rights Watch, this was – in addition to Prudence Bushnell's abovementioned plea to "stop killing people" – the only example of high-level attention given to officials involved in the genocide. While recognizing the severity of the slaughter, the 22 April press statement reiterates the US policy of limited involvement despite the recognition that "the horrors of civil war and mass killings of civilians … have shocked and appalled the world community":

> All responsible officials and military officers must bring offending troops and units under control immediately. We call on the Rwandan army and the Rwandan Patriotic Front to agree on an immediate ceasefire and return to negotiations … We applaud the efforts of regional leaders who are actively engaged in the search for peace and call on the people of the region to support their quest. The United States is prepared to participate … in renewed negotiation in the context of the Arusha Agreement …
>
> (White House 1994b)

In late April, a US intelligence analyst noted, "The plan appears to have been to wipe out any RPF ally or potential ally, and thus raise the costs and limit the possibility of an RPF/Tutsi takeover … No end to the unprecedented bloodshed is yet in sight" (US Department of State 1994d). On the same day that this analysis was revealed, a telegram from the Department of State to the US Embassies in Bujumbura and Dar es Salaam urging Colonel Bagosora to end the killings reveals the US government's focus on returning to the Arusha "peace process" while hundreds of thousands were being slaughtered in the streets of Rwanda. US Deputy Assistant Secretary for African Affairs, Prudence Bushnell acknowledged that "in the eyes of the world, the Rwandan military [are] engaged in criminal acts, aiding and abetting civilian massacres" (Frontline 2004).

Beyond avoidance, George Moose, former Assistant Secretary of State for African Affairs, underlines the instrumental role played by the US in blocking an effective response to the genocide. In one of the many examples of bureaucratic inertia and self-serving caution that marked the US response, Moose talks about the "truly shameful episode" where US officials rejected a plan to jam the extremists hate radio broadcasts "because of some legal nicety about international radio conventions. And then the [50 armored personnel carriers] thing … We spent so much time wrangling about who was going to pay for refurbishing them … for transporting them. It's sort of bureaucracy at its very worst, and we couldn't break through that" (US Department of State 1994e).

Thus, despite overwhelming evidence of genocide and knowledge as to its perpetrators, the lack of immediately apparent national economic, geostrategic, or military benefits to the United States resulted in inaction in response to the slaughter in Rwanda. Instead, US officials confined themselves to public statements, diplomatic demarches, initiatives for a ceasefire, and attempts to contact both the interim government perpetrating the killing and RPF. At the United Nations, the US used its influence to discourage a robust UN response (US Department of State 1994b, 1994f). Only after the genocide was over did the US provide substantial support to assist humanitarian relief efforts for those displaced by the genocide (Ferroggiaro 2001). Yet, while the failure to halt the genocide in Rwanda was awful, the lack of response can be understood, given the context within which the crisis emerged and the prevailing notion of the state as a pluralist moral actor at the time. This relational constructivist analysis of the complexity of the situation helps explain why the US rationally arrived at its decision not to intervene and why it construed any moral responsibility in highly restrictive terms.

Early warnings and the United States' rhetorical response: avoiding the term "genocide"

The bureaucratic paralysis in response to the atrocities in Rwanda arguably emerged from the US administration's decision not to intervene. The Clinton administration was determined to avoid the definition of Rwanda as "genocide" out of fear that this commonplace was encoded with an obligation to take action to stop the slaughter. The United States did not want to admit that something was transpiring that would impose a moral, if not legal, obligation to intervene because no public official wanted to – again – explain why American soldiers were dying in faraway Africa, where the United States had no compelling security interests. Seven weeks into the genocide, President Clinton restated his Jeffersonian policy that the US would intervene in a humanitarian crisis only if it was in America's narrowly defined national interest:

> The end of the superpower standoff lifted the lid from a cauldron of long-simmering hatreds. Now the entire global terrain is bloody with such conflicts, from Rwanda to Georgia … Our interests are not sufficiently at stake in so many of them to justify a commitment of our folks … Whether we get involved in any of the world's ethnic conflicts in the end must depend on the cumulative weight of the American interest at stake.
>
> (Frontline 2004)

A Congressional Official responsible for Africa articulated the same point thus: "The United States has no friends. The United States has interests. And in the United States there is no interest in Rwanda … we are not interested in sending young American marines to bring them back in coffins. We have no incentive" (*ibid.*). At the heart of the matter, therefore, was the question of whether the Clinton administration could justify sacrificing American soldiers to protect civilians facing massacre in Rwanda. In light of the recent collapse of the UN mission to Somalia, and mindful of his primary responsibility as president to protect and promote American lives and interests, President Clinton concluded that American interests were not sufficiently at stake in Rwanda to warrant intervention.

Accordingly, cognizant of its solidarist commitment to the Genocide Convention, American officials shunned the use of what became known as "the g-word" as evidence of the Rwandan genocide poured in (Power 2001). Fear that the declaration of genocide would, under the terms of the 1948 Genocide Convention, commit the United States to action, or severely harm US credibility to declare genocide but fail to respond, caused hesitation. The Clinton administration presumed that if they described the atrocities as genocide, "it would be natural – and unwelcome for voters to expect that the response would include dispatching troops." A discussion paper on Rwanda testifies to the nature of official thinking:

Genocide Investigation: Language that calls for an international investigation of human rights abuses and possible violations of the genocide convention. Be Careful. [The Office of the] Legal [adviser] at [the] State [Department] was worried about this yesterday – [a] Genocide finding could commit USG [the US government] to actually "do something."

(US Department of Defense 1994b)

This statement along with the goals, options, and tactics addressed in the discussion paper reflects the attitude among officials charged with the day-to-day responsibility for the Rwanda crisis. It reveals the tension associated with the US government's commitment to the Genocide Convention and its relation to what constitutes the "US national interest." It reflects a government aware of its solidarist commitments to the Genocide Convention, yet striving to act based on a pluralist understanding of moral responsibility as limited primarily to American citizens. The discussion paper is filled with cautions against the US committing to action in Rwanda.

The genocide debate in US government circles began the last week of April, but it was not until 21 May, six weeks after the killings began, that Secretary Christopher gave his diplomats permission to publicly declare that "acts of genocide" had occurred:

The delegation is authorized to agree to a resolution that states that "acts of genocide" have occurred in Rwanda or that "genocide has occurred in Rwanda." Other formulations that suggest that some, but not all of the killings in Rwanda are genocide ... e.g. "genocide is taking place in Rwanda" – are authorized. Delegation is not authorized to agree to the characterization of any specific incident as genocide or to agree to any formulation that indicates that all killings in Rwanda are genocide.

(Frontline 2004)

Recognizing the power of its solidarist commitment to the Genocide Convention, the Clinton administration assumed that invoking the term "genocide" would engender expectations of a response that would include dispatching troops, which carries enormous responsibility. By avoiding engagement with rhetorical commonplaces urging action in response to the Rwandan genocide, the Jeffersonian Clinton administration reinforced the state as a pluralist moral actor, bolstering expectations of its accompanying limited notion of moral responsibility in international affairs.

Christine Shelly, a State Department spokesperson, had long been charged with publicly articulating the US position on whether events in Rwanda constituted genocide. Her exchange on 10 June with the Reuters correspondent Alan Elsner exemplifies her attempts at avoiding the term:

> ELSNER: How would you describe the events taking place in Rwanda?
>
> SHELLY: Based on the evidence we have seen from observations on the ground, we have every reason to believe that acts of genocide have occurred in Rwanda.
>
> ELSNER: What's the difference between "acts of genocide" and "genocide"?
>
> SHELLY: Well, I think the – as you know, there's a legal definition of this ... clearly not all of the killings that have taken place in Rwanda are killings to which you might apply that label ... But as to the distinctions between the words, we're trying to call what we have seen so far as best as we can; and based, again, on the evidence, we have every reason to believe that acts of genocide have occurred.
>
> ELSNER: How many acts of genocide does it take to make genocide?
>
> SHELLY: Alan, that's just not a question that I'm in a position to answer.
>
> (Frontline 2004)

In response to a follow-up question, Shelly responded,

> [T]here is a reason for the selection of words that we have made, and I have – perhaps I have – I'm not a lawyer. I don't approach this from the international legal and scholarly point of view. We try, best as we can, to accurately reflect a description in particularly addressing that issue. It's – the issue is out there. People have obviously been talking about it.
>
> (Frontline 2004)

Commenting on Shelly's press conference exchange, journalist Philip Gourevitch summarizes the situation thus:

> She [Shelly] meant that if it was a genocide, the Convention of 1948 required the contracting parties to act. Washington didn't

want to act. So Washington pretended that it wasn't a genocide. Still, assuming that the above exchange took about two minutes, an average of eleven Tutsis were exterminated in Rwanda while it transpired.

(Gourevitch 1999: 153)

From the point of view of a policy that sought to avoid US involvement in either peacekeeping or enforcement operations in Rwanda, the US decision to consciously avoid the inflammatory rhetoric of genocide makes sense, even if it is morally repugnant. Administration officials were probably correct to assume that both the domestic and international public would focus on the strong moral obligation to "never again" allow genocide to occur by pairing the concepts of "genocide" with an international "responsibility to protect." Thus, as Heinze (2007) suggests, while the pressure on the administration to name the crime was intense, if it did so, administration officials reasoned, the pressure to intervene would be even more intense, particularly since the United States is one of the few countries with the assets to execute such an emergency intervention. Consequently, if Somalia was any indication, the political risks of not acting were less than the political risks of acting, and the Clinton administration had much to lose and little to gain from an intervention in the heart of Africa. Since naming the crime would have pressured the United States to act, the US government remained silent. In a back-handed kind of way, therefore, it seems that the solidarist commitment of the Clinton administration was as determinative in US decision-making as its Jeffersonian reluctance to engage. Thus, the US's lack of response to the Rwandan genocide challenged the Clinton administration's own pluralist limited notion of moral responsibility in international relations, generating questions about how to relate to similar situations of severe human rights violations in the future.

The absence of domestic criticism

A July 1994 PIPA survey found that 80 percent of respondents favored intervention if a UN commission had concluded that genocide was occurring in Rwanda (Kull 2004). This finding confirmed the US government's expectation that the deployment and pairing of these rhetorical commonplaces would have afforded action to stop the genocide. For the Jeffersonian Clinton administration, however, motivated by a pluralist limited understanding of the state as a moral actor, domestic policy was the priority. Accordingly, the Rwanda issue (like Bosnia) was perceived more as a threat to the legislative agenda and approval ratings at home than an opportunity to demonstrate international leadership on humanitarian issues. The overarching concern was that referring to the situation in Rwanda as genocide would cause demands for a US response that the administration was not prepared to undertake. By avoiding the rhetoric of genocide, the administration hoped to evade expectations of humanitarian intervention as an activity of the state.

At the time, this strategy was effective. Virtually no constituencies in the United States gave the Clinton administration the impression that it would pay a political price for failing to rescue the Rwandans; and part of the reason for avoiding the rhetoric of genocide was to keep it this way. Domestic political forces that might have pressed for action were absent. And most US officials opposed to American involvement in Rwanda were firmly convinced that they were doing all they could – and, most importantly, all they should – in light of competing American interests and a highly circumscribed understanding of what was "possible" for the US to do (Power 2001). The administration was content with the lack of opposition to their response to Rwanda. At a meeting on the crisis, President Clinton reportedly asked his staff if the Congressional Black Caucus had agitated at all on the issue, and was told that they had not. Accordingly, when a representative from Human Rights Watch asked National Security Adviser Anthony Lake how to make progress in influencing US policy, Lake answered, "Make more noise" (cited in Ronayne 2001: 174).

Paradoxically, then, US officials "simultaneously believed that the American people would oppose US military intervention [in Rwanda] and feared that the public might support intervention if they realized genocide was underway" (Power 2003: 163). This indeed proved to be true, as it was only after the revelation of genocide that it became possible to identify a constituency for action in Rwanda (Gordon 1994). After the genocide had been committed, Senator Paul Simon famously said, "If every member of the House and Senate had received 100 letters from people back home saying we have to do something about Rwanda, when the crisis was first developing, then I think the response would have been different" (Simon 2006).

While not loud enough to change the administration's policy on Rwanda, the White House did face criticism for its word games and diplomatic evasions. Commenting on the Administration's position following a visit to refugee camps in Tanzania, representative Tony P.

Hall (cited in Ronayne 2001: 110) stated, "I believe it is genocide and we need to stop sitting on the sidelines." He continued, "They keep avoiding calling it genocide because they know that as a ratifier [of the UN Genocide Convention] we are required by international law to find the parties responsible and go after them. We need to go after the people who are guilty. We know who they are" (*ibid.*). Similarly, in a 10 June 1994 letter to Clinton, Human Rights Watch President Kenneth Roth explained that since the killing began, "only 4 days ago, Human Rights Watch/Africa has gathered evidence that perhaps as many as 500,000 helpless civilians, mostly of the Tutsi minority, have been slaughtered. How can this be anything but genocide?" (Roth 1994). Moreover, former Bush administration Secretary of State for African Affairs Herman Cohen, in an op-ed in the *Washington Post*, denounced the Clinton administration for its "current wimpish approach to the genocide in Rwanda" and said, "If anything is going to destroy the credibility of the international community in the area of conflict resolution, the American policy is going to do it" (Cohen 1994). Cohen concluded: "another Holocaust may have just slipped by, hardly noticed" (*ibid.*). In the years to follow, it became excruciatingly clear that it had.

However, in the absence of adequate public activism for action, the government did not feel compelled to act. As far as US officials in the Clinton Administration were concerned, there was no political cost to inaction against the Rwandan genocide, as opposed to a potentially steep price to embroilment in yet another violent African quagmire. This appears to have been the final determination of US policy toward Rwanda, even as the human cost of inaction became devastatingly clear (Colgan 2006).

Post-genocide response and its implications for the state as a moral actor

By the end of July 1994, nearly two million Hutus fled Rwanda for safety, spawning the growth of refugee camps in neighboring countries (BBC 2004). As thousands died of disease and starvation in these refugee camps, Clinton ordered airdrops of food and supplies for the Hutu refugees, including known genocidaires. In July, he sent 200 non-combatant troops to Kigali to manage the airport and distribute relief supplies. These troops were subsequently withdrawn by October 1994. Clinton and the United Nations faced criticism for their lack of response to the genocide.

In March of 1998 (the precise date is not available), on a visit to Rwanda, President Clinton issued a carefully hedged declaration, later to be known as the "Clinton apology." Speaking to the crowd assembled at Kigali Airport, he said: "We come here today partly in recognition of the fact that we in the United States and the world community did not do as much as we could have and should have done to try to limit what occurred" in Rwanda. He continued:

> It may seem strange to you here, especially the many of you who lost members of your family, but all over the world there were people like me sitting in offices, day after day after day, who did not fully appreciate [pause] the depth [pause] and the speed [pause] with which you were being engulfed by this unimaginable terror.
>
> (Clinton 1998)

Despite the inaction of the United States during the genocide in Rwanda, this subsequent expression of public contrition as well as the administration's humanitarian assistance to address its aftermath and efforts at accountability and justice carried significant norm-building potential. Emerging out of the relationship between the historical context of the Clinton administration, the choices made in practice by a government rooted in the Jeffersonian ideological foreign policy tradition, and the discourse invoked to justify these actions, was a new understanding of the role of the state as a moral actor. In the process, what was widely considered an appropriate norm – the principle of state sovereignty and non-intervention – was re-interpreted as something that is potentially wrong or immoral; standing by while genocide unfolds. By stating his "apology" in the aforementioned way, Clinton undermined the pluralist normative foundations of his own administration's practices by delegitimizing the beliefs on which they were based and by manipulating the frames within which his policies and practices were viewed.

Much literature on norm development suggests that norm progression commonly results from successful arguments; arguments which Crawford defines as those able to persuade actors to see a state's actions as legitimate or to adopt a specific course of action. In this view, "arguments are less likely to be persuasive if the social and material contexts do not align with the argument" (Crawford 2002: 37). Yet, as Badescu and Weiss (2010) demonstrate, instances when the argument and context are misaligned can help advance norms too. Since "norms and practice are mutually constitutive" (Keck and Sikkink 1998: 35), assessing normative shifts not only through outcomes but also of contestation, can shed light on consolidation. Badescu and Weiss explain, for example, that contestation triggered by misuse has helped advance a solidarist expanded notion of moral responsibility in international relations by fostering necessary clarification. They suggest that "along with positive precedents, misrepresentations clearly falling outside the norm's legitimate scope ... represent alternative paths to norm formation; they too contribute to building a consistent ... message by clarifying what the concept is, and is not" (Badescu and Weiss 2010: 360). In the case of Rwanda, the pairing of commonplaces not recognized as legitimate by the audiences toward which it was directed served to strengthen the relationship between concepts that would warrant action in future cases of genocide, thus altering perceptions of the state as a moral actor. While arguably not powerful enough, the public apologies by the president and the secretary of state following the Rwandan genocide were important milestones in the development of a norm based on an expanded notion of moral responsibility to prevent and punish future genocides.

The Clinton apology recognized not only that they did not do what they *could* have done but also that they did not do what they *should* have done, urging a different response by the US government when faced with similar situations in the future. The US government's struggle to reconcile its pluralist and solidarist commitments in response to Rwanda brought the central question of any normative international theory to the forefront of the agenda, namely the moral value to be attributed to particularistic political collectivities against humanity taken as a while, or the claims of individual human beings. To compensate for the 1994 ban on the word "genocide," Clinton invoked it 11 times in his Rwanda speech, explicitly declaring, "Never again must we be shy in the face of evidence" (Clinton 1998). This statement significantly impacted the international community's collective understanding of the state as a moral actor, and of how far moral responsibility should extend in international relations.

Note

1 The recognition that Rwanda met the definition of "genocide" is evidenced by the existence of the International Criminal Tribunal for Rwanda (ICTR), the purpose of which is to try individuals for the crimes of genocide, crimes against humanity, and certain war crimes (ICTR 1994).

References

Annan, K.A. (1999) Address to the General Assembly. UN press release Sg/Sm/7136, 20 September. New York: United Nations.

Badescu, C.G. and Weiss, T.G. (2010) Misrepresenting R2P and Advancing Norms: An Alternative Spiral? *International Studies Perspective* 11: 354–374.

Barnett, M. (1997) The Politics of Indifference at the United Nations: The Security Council, Peacekeeping, and Genocide in Rwanda. *Cultural Anthropology* 12(1): 551–578.

BBC (2004) Frustration of Darfur "Observer." 14 November. Available at http://news.bbc.co.uk/1/hi/programmes/panorama/4007117.stm (accessed 12 January 2015).

Bloch-Elkon, Y. (2007) Studying the Media, Public Opinion, and Foreign Policy in International Crises: The United States and the Bosnian Crisis 1992–1995. *Harvard International Journal of Press/Politics* 12(4): 20–51.

Burkhalter, H. (1994–1995) The Question of a Genocide: The Clinton Administration and Rwanda. *World Policy Journal* 11(4).

CBS (1994) Interview with Robert Dole. *Face the Nation*, 10 April.

Claes, W. (1994) Letter from the Minister of Foreign Affairs of Belgium to the UN Secretary-General Expressing Concern that Worsening situation in Rwanda May Impede UNAMIRs Capacity to Fulfill Its Mandate. In B. B. Ghali (ed.), *United Nations and Rwanda 1993–1996*. New York: Department of Public Information, United Nations.

Clinton, B. (1998) The Clinton Apology. Available at www.highbeam.com/doc/1G1-20969090.html (accessed 6 July 2009).

Cohen, H. (1994) Getting Rwanda Wrong. *Washington Post*, June 3. Available at www.gpo.gov/fdsys/pkg/CREC-1994-06-10/html/CREC-1994-06-10-pt1-PgS35.htm (accessed 4 April 2010).

Colgan, A. (2006) A Tale of Two Genocides: The Failed US Responses to Rwanda and Darfur. *Peacework Magazine* 33(369): 16–17.

Crawford, N. (2002) *Argument and Change in World Politics*. Cambridge: Cambridge University Press.

Ferroggiaro, W. (2001) The US and the Genocide in Rwanda 1994: Evidence of Inaction. Available at www.gwu.edu/~nsarchiv/NSAEBB/NSAEBB53/index.html (accessed 3 July 2009).

Frontline (1998) Ambush in Mogadishu. *Frontline* season 16, episode 13, first broadcast 29 September. Available at www.pbs.org/wgbh/pages/frontline/shows/ambush/etc/synopsis.html (accessed 12 May 2011).

—— (2004) Ghosts of Rwanda. *Frontline* season 22, episode 6, first broadcast 1 April. Available at www.pbs.org/wgbh/pages/frontline/shows/ghosts (accessed 3 September 2010).

Gordon, M.R. (1994) US to Supply 60 Vehicles for UN Troops in Rwanda. *New York Times*, 16 June. Available at www.nytimes.com/1994/06/16/world/us-to-supply-60-vehicles-for-un-troops-in-rwanda.html (accessed 12 January 2015).

Gourevitch, P. (1999) *We Wish to Inform You that Tomorrow We Will be Killed with Our Families: Stories from Rwanda.* New York: Picador.

Haass, R.N. (1997) *The Reluctant Sheriff: The United States After the Cold War.* New York: Council on Foreign Relations.

Heinze, E. (2007) The Rhetoric of Genocide in US Foreign Policy: Rwanda and Darfur Compared. *Political Science Quarterly* 122(3): 359–383.

Hentoff, N. (1999) The Triumph of Evil. *The Village Voice* (2 March). Available at www.villagevoice.com/1999-03-02/news/the-triumph-of-evil (accessed 19 January 2015).

Human Rights Watch (1999) *Leave None to Tell the Story: Genocide in Rwanda.* New York: Human Rights Watch.

ICTR (1994) United Nations Security Council Resolution 955 Establishing the International Tribunal for Rwanda. Adopted by the Security Council at its 3453rd meeting, 8 November. UN Doc. S/RES/955. Available at http://daccess-ods.un.org/TMP/7914921.04530334.html (accessed 12 January 2015).

Incore (1993) Peace Agreement between the Government of the Republic of Rwanda and the Rwandese Patriotic Front. Available at www.incore.ulst.ac.uk/services/cds/agreements/pdf/rwan1.pdf (accessed 7 April 2011).

Keane, F. (1995) *Season of Blood: A Rwandan Journey.* Harmondsworth: Viking Penguin.

Keating, C. (2004) Rwanda: An Insiders Account. In D. Malone (ed.), *The UN Security Council: from the Cold War to the 21st Century,* 500–512. Boulder, CO: Lynne Rienner Publishers.

Keck, M. and Sikkink, K. (1998) *Activists Beyond Borders.* Ithaca, NY: Cornell University Press.

Khadiagala, G.M. (2001) *National Intelligence Project on Intervention in Internal Conflict: the Case of Rwanda.* Available at www.cissm.umd.edu/papers/files/rwanda.pdf (accessed 7 March 2011).

Kull, S. (2004) *Americans on the Crisis in Sudan.* Washington, DC: Program on International Policy Attitudes (PIPA). Available at www.pipa.org/OnlineReports/Africa/Sudan_Jul04/Sudan_Jul04_rpt.pdf (accessed 3 March 2010).

Lebor, A. (2006) *Complicity with Evil: The United Nations in the Age of Modern Genocide.* Harrisburg, VA: R.R. Donnelley.

Lewis, P. (1994) UN Backs Troops for Rwanda but Terms Bar Any Action Soon. *New York Times,* 17 May. Available at www.nytimes.com/1994/05/17/world/un-backs-troops-for-rwanda-but-terms-bar-any-action-soon.html (accessed 12 January 2015).

McFadden, R. (1994) Western Troops Arrive in Rwanda to Aid Foreigners. *New York Times,* 2 April. Available at www.nytimes.com/1994/04/10/world/western-troops-arrive-in-rwanda-to-aid-foreigners.html (accessed 12 January 2015).

Mead, W.R. (2002) *Special Providence.* New York: Routledge.

Melvern, L. and Williams, P. (2004) Britannia Waived the Rules: The Major Government and the 1994 Genocide. *African Affairs* 103: 1–22.

Military.com (2009) Overview of the US Intervention in Somalia. 24 September. Available at www.military.com/NewContent/0,13190,NI_ Somalia_0104,00.html (accessed 6 June 2010).

National Security Council Project (2000) *Oral History Roundtables: The Clinton Administration.* 27 September. Washington, DC: The Brookings Institution. Available at www.brookings.edu/about/projects/archive/ nsc/20000927 (accessed 12 January 2015).

OAU (1998) OAU Sets Inquiry into Rwanda Genocide. *Africa Recovery* 12(1): 4. Available at www.un.org/ecosocdev/geninfo/afrec/subjindx/121rwan.htm (accessed 11 February 2010).

Otiti, A. K. (2010) Media and the Rwanda Genocide. Available at www.themediaproject.org/article/cam-media-rwanda-genocide (accessed 4 May 2011).

Parmalee, J. (1994) Fade to Blood: Why the International Answer to the Rwandan Atrocities is Indifference. *Washington Post*, 24 April: C3.

Power, S. (2001) Bystanders to Genocide: Why the United States Let the Rwandan Tragedy Happen. *Atlantic Monthly*, September. Available at www.theatlantic.com/magazine/archive/2001/09/bystanders-to-geno-cide/304571 (accessed 19 January 2015).

—— (2003) *A Problem from Hell: America in the Age of Genocide.* New York: Harper Perennial.

Richburg, K.B. (1994) Westerners Begin Feeling Rwanda; 170 Americans Leave by Convoy. *The Washington Post*, 10 April. Available at www.highbeam.com/doc/1P2-884897.html (accessed 19 January 2015).

Ronayne, P. (2001) *Never Again? The United States and the Prevention and Punishment of Genocide.* Lanham, MD: Rowman & Littlefield Publishers.

Roth, K. (1994) *Human Rights in Africa and US Policy.* New York: Human Rights Watch.

Simon, P. (2006) Congressional Record – Senate, vol. 152, pt. 17, 6 December.

UN (1951) Convention on the Prevention and Punishment of the Crime of Genocide. Adopted by Resolution 260 (III) of the UN General Assembly (9 December 1948). UN Treaty Series no. 1021, 78(277). Available at www.preventgenocide.org/law/convention/text.htm (accessed 6 September 2009).

UN Economic and Social Council (1993) Question of the Violation of Human Rights and Fundamental Freedoms in any Part of the World, with Particular Reference to Colonial and Other Dependent Countries and Territories. Commission on Human Rights fiftieth session. UN doc. E/CN.4/1994/7/Add.1. Available at www.preventgenocide.org/prevent/ UNdocs/ndiaye1993.htm (accessed 13 October 2009).

UN Security Council (1999) *Report of the Independent Inquiry into the Actions of the United Nations during the 1994 Genocide in Rwanda.* 15 December. Available at www.securitycouncilreport.org/atf/cf/%7B65BFCF9B-6D27-

4E9C-8CD3-CF6E4FF96FF9%7D/POC%20S19991257.pdf (accessed 7 March 2011).

US Defense Intelligence Agency (1994) *Rwanda: The Rwandan Patriotic Fronts Offensive*. 9 May. Washington, DC: US Defense Intelligence Agency.

US Department of Defense (1994a) Office of the Deputy Assistant Secretary of Defense for Middle East/Africa Region. Drafted by Lt. Col. Michael Harvin. Circa 11 May. Rwanda Interagency Telecon.

—— (1994b) Discussion Paper. Office of the Deputy Assistant Secretary of Defense for Middle East/Africa Region (1 May). Available at www.gwu.edu/~nsarchiv/NSAEBB/NSAEBB53/rw050194.pdf (accessed 22 April 2009).

US Department of State (1994a) US Deputy Assistant Secretary of Defense for Middle East Africa. *Talking Points on Rwanda–Burundi* (11 April). Available at http://repositories.lib.utexas.edu/bitstream/handle/2152/5674/2276.pdf?sequence=1 (accessed 19 January 2015).

—— (1994b) Cable number 099440, to US Mission to the United Nations, New York. 15 April. Available at www.gwu.edu/~nsarchiv/NSAEBB/NSAEBB53/ (accessed 6 May 2010).

—— (1994c) Bureau of African Affairs. Memorandum from Deputy Assistant Secretary of State Prudence Bushnell to the Secretary through Under Secretary for Political Affairs Peter Tarnoff. Death of Rwandan and Burundian Presidents in Plane Crash Outside Kigali, 6 April. Available at www.gwu.edu/~nsarchiv/NSAEBB/NSAEBB53/rw040694.pdf (accessed 7 March 2009).

—— (1994d) Cable number 113672, to US Embassy Bujumbura and US Embassy Dar es Salaam, DAS. Bushnell Tells Col. Bagosora to Stop the Killings. 29 April. Available at www.gwu.edu/~nsarchiv/NSAEBB/NSAEBB53/rw042994.pdf (accessed 2 May 2011).

—— (1994e) Rwanda: Jamming Civilian Radio Broadcasts. Memorandum from Under Secretary of Defense for Policy to Deputy Assistant to the President for National Security, National Security Council. 5 May.

—— (1994f) Cable number 127262, to US Mission to the United Nations, New York. Rwanda: Security Council Discussions. 13 May. Available at www.gwu.edu/~nsarchiv/NSAEBB/NSAEBB53/rw051394.pdf (accessed 6 May 2011).

US Embassy in Kigali (1994) Cable to the Secretary of State, Washington DC. DAS Bushnell meets Habyarimana and RPF. Confidential. Available at www.gwu.edu/~nsarchiv/NSAEBB/NSAEBB117/Rw01.pdf (accessed 8 August 2011).

US House Foreign Affairs Committee (1994) Hearing of the International Security, International Organization and Human Rights Sub-committee of the House Foreign Relations Committee. 103rd Congress, 2nd session.

Vetlesen, A. J. (2000) Genocide: A Case for the Responsibility of the Bystander. *Journal of Peace Research* 37(4): 519–532.

White House (1994a) Presidential Decision Directive: PDD 25. 5 May. Office of the Press Secretary. Available at www.fas.org/irp/offdocs/pdd25.htm (accessed 8 September 2009).

—— (1994b) Statement by the Press Secretary. 22 April. Washington, DC: The White House.

—— (1993) Press Briefing by Secretary of State Warren Christopher, Secretary of Defense Les Aspin and Admiral David Jeremiah. 7 October. Online by Gerhard Peters and John T. Woolley, The American Presidency Project. Available at www.presidency.ucsb.edu/ws/?pid=60014 (accessed 19 January 2015).

3   The US response to Darfur

> The brutal treatment of innocent civilians in Darfur is unacceptable
> – it is unacceptable to me, it is unacceptable to Americans, it's
> unacceptable to the United Nations. This status quo must not
> continue.
>
> (George W. Bush 2007)

Conflict in the Darfur region of Sudan broke out in 2003 when the government unleashed the Sudanese military and Janjaweed militia to attack
civilians in response to a rebellion by marginalized groups, namely the
Sudan Liberation Movement (or Sudan Liberation Army) and the Justice
and Equality Movement. By 2007, the conflict had led to the death of
more than 400,000 civilians in Darfur, displacing over two million
(Prunier 2007). The US government was quick to invoke the term "genocide" to describe the atrocities, thus relying on this rhetorical
commonplace to give the impression that they, unlike the Clinton administration a decade earlier, took a firm stance against "crimes against
humanity." However, the subsequent conclusion by the 2005 UN
Commission of Inquiry on Darfur that genocide had not taken place molli-
fied expectations of forceful action in accordance with the UN Genocide
Convention (UN 1951) and the emerging responsibility to protect (R2P)
doctrine (ICISS 2001).[1] In contrast to the Clinton administration, therefore, the George W. Bush administration found itself in an environment in
which it could deploy rhetorical commonplaces that would have
warranted forceful military intervention in the case of Rwanda ten years
earlier. At the same time, it could justify inaction by referencing the political climate at the time. Questioning the pairing of rhetorical
commonplaces such as "situations of genocide" with a "responsibility to
protect" and the "national interest," this approach was compatible with the
Bush administration's understanding that the declaration of genocide did

not necessarily imply an obligation to intervene. Relying on skepticism toward the government's Jacksonian foreign policy to justify the deployment of the rhetoric of genocide as a substitute for more decisive action, the discourse on genocide was utilized instrumentally by the Bush administration to avoid engagement in the Darfur conflict as well as the stigma associated with standing by while genocide unfolds.

This relational constructivist case study suggests that the Bush administration's strategic deployment of the rhetoric of the Genocide Convention and the emerging R2P doctrine was indicative of a solidarist expanded notion of moral responsibility gaining increased recognition in international relations, compelling the Bush administration to reference an international "responsibility to protect" in response to "genocide." Yet, it also exposes the tension generated by this development, and the US government's struggle to employ this rhetoric while reinforcing its commitment to a limited, pluralist understanding of the state as a moral actor. Instead, while employed instrumentally by the pluralist Jacksonian Bush administration, the rhetorical commonplaces evoked in the case of Darfur added force to the emerging solidarist expanded notion of moral responsibility in international relations. Attributing the state with a moral responsibility to speak and act consistently in defense of human rights independently of national borders, the Bush administration undermined its own pluralist foundation by strengthening expectations of the US to react in response to similar situations of human rights violations in the future.

The Bush Doctrine: from Jeffersonianism to Jacksonianism

The Wilsonian disappointment

The appalling atrocities of the wars in the 1990s, and the failure of the international community to take earlier, stronger, and more effective steps against persecution of entire populations, brought many Wilsonians to the conclusion that the prevention of future carnage of this kind would be a central and inescapable moral duty of the United States. "Never again" was assumed to become one of the basic principles of US foreign policy. The emergence of the concept of the R2P in the late 1990s gained acceptance for the idea of humanitarian intervention as a legitimate use of military force. The pairing of these commonplaces with the concept of "the national interest" was interpreted as a move in the direction of a solidarist, expanded notion of the state as a moral actor.

However, to the Wilsonians' great disappointment and surprise, popular enthusiasm for military intervention remained limited despite the success of the NATO intervention in Kosovo in 1999. The genocide in Rwanda; the civil conflicts in Sudan and Somalia; the breakdown of order in failed states like Sierra Leone; the Russian war against the Chechens; and the international war in the Congo, did not persuade the American public to back a consistent strategy of humanitarian intervention – either alone or with the UN. While support for response existed, the contested nature of the normative space in which questions related to humanitarian interventions emerged revealed that revulsion against these atrocities did not automatically translate into political will to put American forces in harm's way to protect the lives of civilians in remote locations. By the end of the twentieth century, Wilsonians were coming to realize that the key constraints on their ability to build the global order based on a solidarist notion of moral responsibility they had long sought, did not come from hostile external powers but from their limited political resources within the United States. The same forces that blocked United States membership in Wilson's League and that kept the United States out of the Permanent Court of Justice in the 1920s were still capable of blocking Wilsonian initiatives early in the twenty-first century. Wilsonians simply lacked the domestic political strength to implement their foreign policy in a consistent, effective manner (Mead 2002).

Accordingly, when Bush took office in 2000, defending human rights abroad ranked low on the list of public priorities for American foreign policy. While most agreed that these ethnic slaughters were tragic, from the standpoint of a majority of the American people, motivated by a pluralist limited notion of moral responsibility in international relations, it was considered preferable to have numerous slaughters in progress than to have American troops risk their lives in a number of disintegrating trouble spots around the world (*ibid.*). In the presidential debate on 12 October 2000 (PBS 2000), Bush stated his priority: "The first question is what's in the best interest of the United States? What's in the best interest of our people?" Responding to popular opinion, Bush stressed the difference between his Jeffersonian foreign policy and the alleged excess of "Clintonian globalism," citing the Clinton intervention in Haiti as an example of unnecessary deployment of American troops. Returning the focus to domestic politics, Bush's campaign hinted that his administration would seek to withdraw American forces from Kosovo. Protesting against the Clinton administration's support for financial institutions like the International Monetary Fund and the

World Bank, he expounded his view of the United Nations as little more than "an opportunity for people to vent" (Allen 2000).

9/11: changing politics and policies

When elected to the American presidency in 2000, Bush gave every indication that he, like his father before him to a certain extent, was a conventional "realist," committed to a Jeffersonian grand strategy of selective engagement. He was critical of the open-ended nature of the Clinton doctrine and of what he described as its "indiscriminate use of military force" in instances not involving vital national interests (Owens 2006). Adopting themes from Jeffersonianism, he emphasized the need for the United States to lower its profile, to walk more "humbly," and to move back to a narrower and more restricted perspective of the national interest, viewing foreign policy not simply as a field of concern in its own right but as an instrument of domestic policy (PBS 2000). In his speeches, Bush stressed foreign policy retrenchment and military "transformation" in preparation for the emergence of a future power balancer similar to that of the Soviet Union during the Cold War. Neither Bush nor his advisers, most notably national security adviser Condoleezza Rice and Secretary of State Colin Powell, spoke of spreading democracy throughout the world. On the contrary, Bush declared:

> I'm not so sure the role of the United States is to go around the world and say this is the way it's got to be. We can help. And maybe it's just our difference in government, the way we view government. I mean I want to empower people. I want to help people help themselves, not have government tell people what to do. I just don't think it's the role of the United States to walk into a country and say, "we do it this way, so should you."
>
> (PBS 2000)

Following the terrorist attacks of 9/11, however, the president abandoned his Jeffersonianism and embraced a Jacksonian approach to foreign affairs. 9/11 significantly lowered the level of threat that Washington was prepared to accept without engaging in an active response, encouraging a more widespread preference among Western governments for pursuing policies involving action rather than restraint. Further, 9/11 highlighted the vulnerability of Western cities to the scenario of an al-Qaida cell armed with weapons of mass destruction. Moreover, 9/11 reinforced the argument that the US and its allies were facing a new type of enemy: a globalized network of insurgents who ignored the laws of war and reveled in trying to cause as much fear and carnage as possible (Heinze 2007). These effects of 9/11 led to a rethinking of US grand strategy and the emergence of what became known as "the Bush Doctrine."

The main elements of the emergent "Bush Doctrine" were delineated in the National Security Strategy of the United States published on 20 September 2002. It was stated as follows in the updated version published in 2006:

> The security environment confronting the United States today is radically different from what we have faced before. Yet the first duty of the United States Government remains what it always has been: to protect the American people and American interests. It is an enduring American principle that this duty obligates the govern-ment to participate and counter threats, using all elements of national power, before the threats can do grave damage. The greater the threat, the greater the risk of inaction – and the more compelling the case for taking anticipatory action to defend ourselves, even if uncertainty remains as to the time and place of the enemy's attack. There are few greater threats than a terrorist attack with WMD [weapons of mass destruction].
>
> To forestall or prevent such hostile acts by our adversaries, the United States will, if necessary, act preemptively in exercising our inherent right of self-defense. The United States will not resort to force in all cases to preempt emerging threats. Our preference is that nonmilitary actions succeed. And no country should ever use preemption as a pretext for aggression.
>
> (White House 2002)

The Bush Doctrine has been defined as a collection of strategy princi-ples, practical policy decisions, and a set of rationales and ideas for guiding United States policy. Its two main pillars are promoting demo-cratic regime change and the possibility of pre-emptive strikes against potential enemies. Nesting the US within the broader community of "the West" following 9/11, the Bush administration declared that the United States was entangled in a global war of ideas between the Western values of freedom on the one hand, and extremism seeking to destroy them, on the other. It was described as a war of ideology where the United States would have to take responsibility for security and show leadership in the world by actively seeking out its enemies and forcefully pursuing change in the countries supporting them. By nesting the US within the broader community of "the West," the Bush administration justified the declared "war on terrorism" by connecting it with broader interests and values beyond the United States. The National Security Strategy document states, "America is now threatened less by conquering states than we are by failing ones. We are menaced less by fleets and armies than by catastrophic technologies in the hands of the embittered few" (*ibid.*). This, it asserted, requires "defending the United States, the American people, and our interests at home and abroad by identifying and destroying the threat before it reaches our borders" (*ibid.*).

As mentioned in Chapter 1, nested community arguments are powerful rhetorical commonplaces because they function as something of a rhetorical trump card when deployed against referencing only a subordinate community, connoting as they do a concern with broader interests and values. In a series of speeches in late 2001 and 2002, Bush utilized this approach to expand his Jacksonian view of American foreign policy and global interventionism. He announced that the United States would actively support democratic governments around the world as a strategy for combating the threat of terrorism. In doing so, he affirmed that the United States would maintain the right to act unilaterally to defend its own security interests, without the approval of international bodies such as the United Nations. In the first Bush–Kerry debate on 30 September 2004, Bush avowed, "My attitude is you take pre-emptive action in order to protect the American people, that you act in order to make this country secure" (Associated Press 2004). In the 2004 State of the Union address (Bush 2004a), he further insisted, "America will never seek a permission slip to defend the security of our country."

While nesting the United States within a larger moral context of "the West," however, the Bush administration simultaneously rejected a general moral equivalency in international affairs. Instead, the Bush Doctrine unapologetically asserts the need for moral judgment in international relations. Interpreting the United States as a superior moral actor, it attributes the right and responsibility to the US government to utilize all foreign policy instruments available to protect and promote American interests and ideals. Drawing on what Robert Kaufman (2007) has called moral democratic realism, the Bush Doctrine holds that liberal democratic regimes are superior to tyrannies and need to be promoted. In this view, economic factors such as poverty and hunger are the "root causes" of terrorism, which is aimed at the destruction of Western liberalism. The remedy is considered to be democratic regime change (Owens 2009). Reinforcing the state as a pluralist moral actor with a corresponding notion of moral responsibility limited to the protection and promotion of American interests and ideals, the Bush Doctrine justified the deployment of extreme measures to meet its objectives. Declaring the US as a superior moral actor in international relations, the net effect of the Bush doctrine was to signal to the rest of the world that America would not be bound by international norms, conventions, and institutions that it perceived as being contrary to its best interests. As the hegemonic power in the post-Cold War era, this US concept of pre-eminence reflected in the Bush doctrine became a factual statement, especially with regard to US military power: the US was clearly the world's pre-eminent actor. However, as a political aspiration that Washington would strive to maintain indefinitely – employing military force as it saw fit – it was interpreted as an offensive stance (Daalder and Lindsay 2003).

Yet, unlike conventional wisdom that the Bush Doctrine represented a radical departure from the past, Mackubin Thomas Owens (2009) observes that, far from being a neoconservative innovation, the Bush Doctrine was in fact well within the mainstream of US foreign policy. While the Bush administration arguably pursued a more aggressive approach to the promotion of national interests than its predecessors, US national interest has always been concerned with more than simple security. It has always had both a commercial and an ideological component (Mead 2002). Moreover, the unilateral notion that Washington does not need an international "permission slip" to engage in action to protect its vital national security interests is a long-standing feature of US foreign policy. Critics of the Bush Doctrine mock its emphasis on expanding liberal democracy as "muscular Wilsonianism." Yet the notion of expansion of like regimes to protect their own can be found in the foundation of foreign policy going back to the writings of Thucydides, who noted that an important goal of both Athens and Sparta was to establish and support regimes similar to their own (Owens 2009). Indeed, the Bush Doctrine endorses this Thucydidean perspective on a global basis. As the president declared during a June 2004 speech at the Air Force Academy:

> Some who call themselves "realists" question whether the spread of democracy in the Middle East should be of any concern of ours. But the realists in this case have lost contact with fundamental reality. America has always been less secure when freedom is in retreat and more secure when freedom is on the march.
>
> (Bush 2004b)

The Bush Doctrine is thus based on the understanding that the security of the United States is enhanced when it is surrounded by other states that share its principles and interests. This belief that the United States has an important national interest in spreading American democratic values throughout the world is shared by Wilsonians, yet the Bush administration's primary motivation of protecting and promoting the physical security and economic well-being of the American people indicates the Jacksonian foundation of the administration's foreign policy. This instrumental motivation is significant to understanding the Bush administration's selective engagement in response to humanitarian catastrophes, as discussed in more detail below.

According to Robert Kagan (2008: n.p.), the expansive, moralistic, militaristic tradition in foreign policy associated with Jacksonianism and the Bush Doctrine, while "checked at times by overseas debacles, or by foreign powers too big and strong to be coerced into acceptance of the American truth," has historically been the dominant approach to achieving this goal. In this view, US foreign policy is "the hearty offspring of this marriage between American's driving ambitions and their overpowering sense of righteousness," motivated by "a steady and determined rise to global dominance" (*ibid.*). From this perspective, the description of the Athenians by the Corinthians in Thucydides' *Peloponnesian War* is applicable to Americans as well: active, innovative, daring, quick, enterprising, acquisitive, and opportunistic. Like the Athenians, Americans "were born into the world to take no rest themselves and to give none to others" (Owens 2009: 40). Accordingly, as Andrew Bacevich (2008: 5), referring to the Iraq war, writes in *The Limits of Power*, "The impulses that have landed us in a war of no exits and no deadlines come from within. Foreign policy has, for decades, provided an outward manifestation of American domestic ambitions, urges, and fears." For Bacevich, the Bush Doctrine represented continuity, not innovation, reflecting "the accumulated detritus of freedom, the by-products of our frantic pursuit of life, liberty, and happiness" (*ibid.*). The commitment to these ideals was exacerbated by the 9/11 attacks, leading to more aggressive strategies in foreign policy. Though it meant following a course that was derided abroad and often criticized at home, Bush was steadfast in his most important trust as president, namely the safety of his citizens (Dale 2008). Thus, in contrast to those attributing foreign policy decisions during the Bush era to the manipulation by wicked individuals or to deception – as was suggested in the case of Iraq – the Bush Doctrine is compatible with the record of the Jacksonian foreign policy tradition.

While aggressive in its approach, however, in the case of the Bush Doctrine, as with the Clinton Doctrine before and the Obama Doctrine after, the main issue in foreign policy was prudence – the weighing of the consequences of alternative political actions (Morgenthau 1948). According to Morgenthau, drawing from Aristotle, prudence is the virtue most characteristic of the statesman. In foreign affairs, prudence requires the statesman to adapt universal principles to particular circumstances, conscious of its potential various outcomes. Representing a continuation of a policy that fuses American security and the "American mission," the Bush administration was selective about the cases in which to intervene on humanitarian grounds. Accordingly, reflecting back at the Clinton administration's decision not to intervene when faced with the genocide in Rwanda, Bush reasoned:

> I think the administration did the right thing in that case. I do. It was a horrible situation. No one liked to see it on our TV screens, but it's a case where we need to make sure we've got an early warning system in places where there could be ethnic cleansing and genocide the way we saw it there in Rwanda. And that's a case where we need to use our influence to have countries in Africa come together and help deal with the situation. The administration made the right decision on training Nigerian troops for situations just such as this in Rwanda. And so I thought they made the right decision not to send US troops into Rwanda.
>
> (Bush 2000)

In this context, the declaration of genocide in Darfur emerged as a puzzle. The Bush administration's unilateral approach would seem to indicate that if they were serious about ending the atrocities in Darfur, they would have found an excuse to intervene unilaterally. However, unlike the Clinton administration ten years earlier, the Bush administration did not understand the declaration of genocide to imply an obligation to intervene according to the UN Genocide Convention and the emerging R2P doctrine. Instead, the rhetoric of genocide was utilized as part of the US administration's strategic deployment to allay concerns by domestic pressure groups related to Sudan's "other civil war," while avoiding engagement in the Darfur conflict as well as the stigma associated with standing by while genocide unfolds. As the following sections demonstrate, the US response to Darfur, while commonly considered to signal the advancement of an expanded notion of moral responsibility in international affairs, more accurately reflects a continued pluralist understanding of the state as a moral actor and its accompanying limited notion of moral responsibility in international relations. Yet the pairing of "situations of genocide" with "a responsibility to protect" utilized by the Bush administration in response to Darfur simultaneously strengthened expectations of forceful action in future cases of severe human rights violations. In this manner, the W. Bush administration contributed to advancing a solidarist expanded notion of moral responsibility in international affairs.

Darfur

> We saw the helicopters bring the soldiers to our village. They killed many people – my father, two of my aunts, my sister, and all her little children.
>
> (Survivor of the Darfur atrocities, cited in Wilson 2006)

Following the 1994 genocide in Rwanda, Power (2001: 104) concluded: "any failure to fully appreciate the genocide stemmed from political, moral, and imaginative weaknesses, not informational ones." Skeptics hold that since 11 September 2001, the United States has even more clearly placed its own strategic interests ahead of concern for human rights, a view supported by the decline in Western contributions to peace operations since 2001. A more optimistic view suggests that intervention can be defensible on grounds of both human rights and national security if a state believes that vital security interests are at stake (Steele 2007). The experience in response to the atrocities in Darfur between 2003 and 2007 suggests not only that the Bush-declared "war on terrorism" fractured the fragile international consensus over humanitarian intervention, but also that the problem of political will bedeviled effective humanitarian intervention as it did over Rwanda.

Compelled by the pressure to "do something" or at least "say something" about Darfur on the 10-year anniversary of the Clinton administration's failure to acknowledge the reality in Rwanda, the Bush administration engaged in the rhetoric of genocide to appease constituencies. However, motivated by a pluralist understanding of the state as a moral actor, the president exploited the political climate at the time to avoid the expectation that the US would participate in military intervention. Despite daily reports on widespread atrocities and grave violations of human rights against the civilian populations in Darfur and the pairing of rhetorical commonplaces affording action, this case illustrates how the promotion of national interest dominated UN Security

Council decision-making. Yet, despite the intent to act according to a pluralist understanding of the state as a moral actor, this relational constructivist analysis also reveals how the pairing of commonplaces such as "genocide" and "the responsibility to protect" with "the national interest" generated expectations of greater consistency in words and actions in future cases of severe human rights violations. The pluralist–solidarist tension reflected in the US response to Darfur, therefore, eventually contributed to advancing an expanded notion of moral responsibility in international affairs.

Background: the emerging threat of genocide and the United Nations' initial response

Darfur is a region in Western Sudan with an estimated pre-conflict population of around 6 million.[2] Land scarcity has fueled competition between the African and Arab Dafurians since Sudan gained independence from Britain and Egypt in 1956 (Steele 2007). The competition intensified with increased scarcity of land and water resources in the 1980s (Prunier 2007: 54–80). Beginning in February 2003, when Darfurian rebels rose up against what they perceived as an increasingly oppressive rule by the Islamic government in Khartoum, a brutal counter-insurgency developed. This created what the UN has described as a "reign of terror" in Darfur (Powell 2004). At least 400,000 people died and over two million were forced from their homes, making Darfur one of the worst series of ongoing human rights violations in the world at the time. The threat of genocide emerged amidst findings that the government's strategy to counter the insurgency was to depopulate the countryside of "sympathetic" Darfurians by arming and providing air support to the Arab Janjaweed militia, who would attack villages, kill, rape, and forcibly displace the civilian population (Human Rights Watch 2004).

While the conflict in Darfur had been raging since February 2003, it took nearly a year for it to emerge as a serious human rights issue in international discourse. Pairing situations of severe human rights violations to the R2P, the popular press and non-governmental organizations (NGOs) were the first to characterize the Darfur killings as genocide (Williams and Bellamy 2005; Reeves 2004; Kristof 2004). In March 2004, the UN representative in Sudan, Mukesh Kapila (2004), identified Darfur as the "world's greatest human rights catastrophe," suggesting that "the only difference between Rwanda and Darfur is the numbers involved." A month later, reinforcing the relationship between the rhetorical commonplaces of genocide and the R2P, former UN Secretary-General Kofi Annan made a direct comparison between the Darfur crisis and the 1994 Rwandan genocide. In this way, Annan attempted to promote a solidarist expanded notion of the state as a moral actor in international affairs. Speaking at the UN Human Rights Commission on the tenth anniversary of the Rwandan genocide, the Secretary-General stated, "whatever term it uses to describe the situation, the international community cannot stand idle … [but] must be prepared to take swift and appropriate action. By action in such situations I mean a continuum of steps, which may include military action" (UN Secretary-General 2004). As the crisis escalated, warnings of imminent disaster multiplied, accompanied by strong rhetoric to merit action. In July, United Nations Secretary-General Kofi Annan warned that the risk of genocide was "frighteningly real" in Darfur (UN 2004). Independent observers noted that the tactics employed, including dismemberment and killing of noncombatants, including young children and babies, resembled the ethnic cleaning used in the Yugoslav wars. The International Crisis Group (BBC 2004) reported in May 2004 that over 350,000 could potentially die as a result of starvation and disease. With the rhetoric of genocide now raised, and with high-profile personalities drawing comparisons between Darfur and the world's dilapidated response to the Rwanda genocide 10 years prior, the international community started to pay closer attention to the events in Darfur (Heinze 2007).

Initially confined to Sudan, the crisis took on an international dimension in April 2004 when over 100,000 refugees poured into neighboring Chad, pursued by Janjaweed militia, clashing with Chadian government forces along the border. Subsequently, in July 2004 – adopted due to China's abstention – the UN declared the conflict a "threat to international peace and security" (UN Security Council 2004a). The UN suggested that the government of Sudan had not met its commitments and expressed concern at helicopter attacks and assaults by the Janjaweed militia against villages in Darfur. The UN concluded in 2005 (UN Commission of Inquiry on Darfur 2005) that the government of Sudan and the Janjaweed were responsible for "crimes against humanity and war crimes [that] may be no less serious and heinous than genocide."

Aiming to mobilize international attention and gain recognition for the severity of the conflict in Darfur, the call for protection in Darfur was, from the beginning, framed within the language of the R2P, which was gaining increased recognition in international discourse at the time.

The R2P, however, failed to activate sufficient political will for states to agree on an explicit and convincing response to the atrocities. Members of the Security Council continued to be divided over the UN's mandate. Their subsequent demands were neither coherent nor accompanied by adequate enforcement mechanisms (Badescu and Bergholm 2009). Due to a lack of understanding of the conditions on the ground, the limited scope of the Darfur Peace Agreement (DPA), signed in May 2006, resulted in failure (International Crisis Group 2007). The Khartoum government did not comply with requirements on facilitating humanitarian access, the disarmament of militias, civilian protection, and the investigation and punishment of human rights violations. Moreover, acting as spoilers in the peace process, signatories to the DPA, especially the Sudan Liberation Army (SLA) faction of Minni Minawi continued to be responsible for attacks on civilians, on the African Union Mission in Sudan (AMIS), and on camps for internally displaced persons. Rebel groups that did not sign the DPA further boycotted talks and increased military action (*ibid.*). Furthermore, Sudanese opposition to the deployment of 18,000 international peacekeepers to replace the 7,000 African Union force, depicting UN intervention as a colonial plan, caused hesitation in the UN Security Council, leaving the R2P in the hands of the African Union (AU). The actions taken by the UN Security Council in delegating the responsibility to the AU are significant as they reflect an awareness of the gravity of the violence in Darfur as well as a level of disagreement among world leaders on how best to proceed when faced with situations of grave human rights violations. Moreover, depicting Darfur as an African problem, this delegation of responsibility indicates an expanded perception of the state as a moral actor with responsibility to protect beyond the state, while maintaining the pluralist notion that geography matters in determining whose responsibility it is to protect civilians from massacre.

The African Union Mission in Sudan and the question of moral agency

Security Council resolution 1769, passed on 31 July 2007, established a hybrid African Union – United Nations Operation in Darfur. In deciding to support a peace operation led by the AU in Darfur, the international community "placed the major burden of response upon the continent least able to marshal the necessary troops, funds, and material to conduct a large-scale civilian-protection operation" (Williams 2006: 178). The African Union Mission in Sudan (AMIS) was the AU's first large-scale military intervention in an internal conflict within one of the Union's own member states. It came well before the AU's new instruments were fully operational, especially those in the East African region (Heinze 2007). The peace and security department of the AU lacked experience in financial accountancy, logistical procurement, and military and defense matters (Badescu and Bergholm 2009). Several of the AU's own members did not contribute to AMIS, leaving the mission over-dependent on external donors' funds and technical advice (International Peace Academy 2007: 4).[3] Nevertheless, the AU was the only multilateral organization with the consent of the Sudanese regime and the will to risk soldiers' lives in Darfur (Badescu and Bergholm 2009). Unfortunately, however, the first 80 African military observers, together with a small protection force of 300 Nigerian and Rwandan troops, arrived in Darfur in June 2004, after the heaviest phase in the killings of civilians was already over (Williams 2006: 176–177, 179).

The delegation of responsibility to the African Union is significant when considering the question of moral agency in international relations and whose responsibility it is to "do something" in the face of massacre. In June 2005, South African President Thabo Mbeki (cited in Rice 2005: B4) suggested, "It's critically important that the African continent should deal with these situations on the continent. And that includes Darfur. ... We have not asked for anybody outside of the African continent to deploy troops in Darfur. It's an African responsibility, and we can do it." However, among the many problems with this position is the question of why events in Darfur should be considered a solely African issue and who would help pay for the deployment of African troops. As mentioned above, although the AU provided the only significant foreign military presence in Darfur until early 2008, AMIS was dependent on external donors for most of its needs and was extremely limited in its ability and willingness to contemplate a robust protection role (Heinze 2007).

Beyond the African continent, the most obvious source of agency was the UN Security Council and its permanent five members in particular, referred to as P5. Yet the Security Council chose not to deploy troops to Darfur without Khartoum's agreement, resulting in inaction. Advocates demanding a tougher response to the atrocities in Darfur used different arguments in attempts to leverage the P5. Having taken a stand on the genocide issue by deploying commonplaces affording action, the United States was implored to not stand idly by in the face of such violence. A similar, although less pronounced set of arguments was made towards the UK, which, under Tony Blair's leadership, had taken a lead role in championing the solidarist expanded notion of moral responsibility and producing the state as a moral actor with a responsibility to protect citizens beyond its own geographical boundaries. France received criticism for not doing more with their military capacity already present in the region. Both China and Russia were requested to stop supplying arms to the Government of Sudan, while China was asked to use its economic relationship with the Sudanese government to persuade al-Bashir's regime to change its policies on Darfur. Outside the Security Council, attention also focused on the activities of self-proclaimed "good international citizens" receptive to the notion of a responsibility to protect independent of national borders, such as Norway and Canada, as well as members of NATO and the European Union. Many of these states had been strong supporters of the solidaristic underpinnings of the Genocide Convention and the R2P, leading to political pressure to give practical effect to these principles in the context of Darfur.

The multiple sources of international action over Darfur highlight the complexity of the question of how far moral responsibility extends in international relations. The Darfur crisis reveals the deep divisions within international society, enabling potential interveners to evade accountability and responsibility by deflecting onto others the "key role" in responding. The resulting political compromise left it to the AU's under-resourced peacekeepers to protect Darfur's civilians and its few ad hoc mediators to take the lead in building a peace process. For the endangered civilians in Darfur it must have seemed as if no one was responsible for their protection. As Paul Williams (2006: 181) has suggested, "For all the money governments spend on their militaries ... the international society is still not prepared to conduct effective responses to mass killings that prioritize the needs of the victims."

Early warnings and the United States' practical response

Unlike in the case of Rwanda, the US arguably tried to rally the UN Security Council into action in response to the atrocities committed in Darfur, urging sanctions against the Khartoum government and deliberately using the term "genocide," requiring action under international law (Shurkin 2005). Under the 2006 Darfur Peace and Accountability Act, Bush strengthened existing sanctions by prohibiting US citizens from engaging in oil-related transactions with Sudan, freezing the assets of complicit parties and denying them entry to the US (Washington Post 2006). The US government facilitated negotiations between rebel groups in an effort to get them to sign a comprehensive peace agreement with the al-Bashir administration and donated 2.4 billion dollars in aid between 2004 and 2007. However, while these efforts are laudable, as Alex Meixner from the Save Darfur Coalition suggests (Voice of America 2007), they amount merely to "keeping people alive so that they can live in terrible conditions in refugee camps," where they are open to attack at any time by both rebels and government soldiers.

Accordingly, as pointed out by Susan Rice (cited in Voice of America 2007), the limited action taken by the US government in response to the Darfur atrocities "is not the approach of a government that is serious about stopping genocide," labeling the US response to Darfur "anemic" and "constipated." In 2006, the UN authorized the deployment of 22,000 UN troops to Darfur, however, instead of imposing the UN soldiers on Sudan, the international community, led by the US, negotiated with the alleged perpetrators in Khartoum for a weaker AU–UN hybrid force – in which UN personnel would take a less active role in peacekeeping, and would mostly provide "logistical support" to the African forces. However, as mentioned above, the AU did not have the capacity to increase its forces from 7,000 to 22,000, nor were they sufficiently trained for such a large operation. Consequently, according to Rice (*ibid.*), "The US government approach and policy has been, over the last three years, one that I have characterized as a pattern of bluster and retreat: They scream loud, they call it genocide, they remonstrate, they bang the table and say this has to stop, they threaten action, and do nothing." She continues, "In effect what we've done ... – we, the international community – is to allow the perpetrators of genocide, the government of Sudan, to dictate the terms of the international community's response to that genocide" (*ibid.*). United States policy-makers have consistently refused to take risks in order to suppress such crimes against humanity (Mayroz 2008: 359). In most cases, the United States has not only objected to the deployment of its ground forces to combat the atrocities, but they have done "almost nothing to deter the crime" (Power 2003: 504).

Early warnings and the United States' rhetorical response: the declaration of genocide as a substitute for more decisive action

Despite this lack of response in practice, the US government was active in addressing the conflict in Darfur in discourse, pairing commonplaces affording action in defense of human rights independent of more narrowly defined national interests. By the summer of 2004, amidst utterances of an impending genocide in Darfur by American evangelicals, African American leaders, and human rights advocates, high-level US officials began to openly refer to the situation as genocide – to the delight of humanitarian interventionists, but to the confusion of students of realpolitik who believed the United States "did not have a dog in that fight" (Washington Post 2004). The first US official to publicly speak of "genocide" in explicit reference to the killings in Darfur was Frank Wolf (R-VA) on 2 April 2004. Members of the Senate, such as Mike DeWine (R-OH), John McCain (R-AZ), and Jon Corzine (D-NJ), subsequently invoked the term numerous times in reference to Darfur (Fessenden 2004a). By June, members on both sides of the aisle began using this strong rhetoric, and on 25 June, a bipartisan roster of 52 Senators sent a letter to Secretary of State Colin Powell urging an increase in assistance to Darfur, targeted sanctions, a travel ban, freezing of assets, and a UN resolution calling for robust monitoring and peacekeeping (*ibid.*). On 22 July 2004, the US House and Senate each passed separate resolutions citing events in Darfur as genocide, calling on the US "administration to continue to lead an international effort to stop genocide," and urging "the administration to seriously consider multilateral or even unilateral intervention to stop genocide in Darfur, Sudan, should the United Nations Security Council fail to act" (H. Con. Res. 467, 108th Cong. 2004; S. Con. Res. 133, 108th Cong. 2004). Two months later, on 9 September 2004, in testimony before the Senate Foreign Relations Committee, the US Secretary of State Colin Powell followed suit, asserting, "we concluded, I concluded, that genocide has been committed in Darfur and that the Government of Sudan and the Jingaweed [*sic*] bear responsibility and that genocide may still be occurring" (Powell 2004).[4] What made this line of reasoning effective was its deployment of existing commonplaces gaining increased recognition at the time, so that the audience toward which the statements were directed recognized the argument as sensible. Subsequently, the British newspaper *The Independent* (Penketh 2005) declared, "At last, Colin Powell uses the word the world's human rights bodies have been demanding as US toughens its stance on the slaughter in Sudan: Genocide." The article concluded that "Branding the atrocities genocide is important as it carries legal and moral obligations under the Genocide Convention" which orders signatories to the Convention "to prevent and punish acts of genocide." Concurrently, the headline of *The Guardian* (MacAskill 2004) that day read, "Stakes Rise as US Declares Darfur Killings Genocide."

Powell's determination led to an American referral of the situation in Darfur to the UN Security Council as part of the United States' legal and moral obligation as a signatory to the Convention on the Prevention and Punishment of the Crime of Genocide to "prevent and punish acts of genocide." This was the first referral of its kind, endorsed shortly after by President Bush (2004c) in a speech in the United Nations. Relating discourse to action, the announcements by Powell and Bush were followed by a strong position taken by the US in the UN Security Council for more forceful action in Darfur.

However, the efforts to brand the atrocities in Darfur genocide did not compel decisive action on the part of the United States or the UN to end the suffering. While Powell and Bush were describing the atrocities in Darfur as genocide, estimates put the number of Darfurians killed per month at around 10,000 (Steele 2007). On 22 April 2004, Samantha Power (2004) testified before the House International Relations Committee that it would require 10,000 troops to effectively stop the killing in Darfur. Only the United States and possibly a few European states have the capacity to rapidly deploy such a force (Prendergast 2004). With massive troop commitments in Iraq and Afghanistan, there was little appetite in Washington for humanitarian intervention, nation building, or other military involvement in Darfur (Associated Press 2004). It would therefore seem unlikely that US officials would rush to volunteer US forces to such a task. The Bush administration would thus seemingly be poorly served by openly referring to the Darfur crisis as genocide if doing so triggers an expectation and obligation to intervene to "prevent and punish" the crime – something the United States did not demonstrate the will to undertake.

According to John Danforth, however, the use of the term "genocide" to describe Darfur was not intended to spur action, but for "internal consumption" to accommodate demands to act by the Christian right (Penketh 2005: 26; see below). In a 27 April press conference, the United States Agency for International Development administrator, Andrew Natsios (2008), revealed – in response to a question related to whether the United States would support a UN-backed humanitarian intervention if the Sudanese government continued to abet the killings in violation of the negotiated ceasefire[5] – that they considered there to be "no alternatives" other than a successful implementation of the ceasefire and that "troops are not going to help us right now." By early July 2004, Defense Department officials revealed that they had no plans to deploy US forces to Darfur any time soon, not even to support the delivery of humanitarian relief (Fessenden 2004b). Even before Congress approved the genocide resolution, Senators Brownback and Corzine had attempted to qualify the language of the resolution by asserting that the purpose of the resolution was not to oblige the United States to intervene in Darfur, but to "add moral weight to efforts to pass a United Nations resolution" (Barker 2004).

It seems clear that from the beginning of the crisis, the Bush administration had little desire to provide material support for peacekeeping or enforcement action in Darfur, much less take it upon itself to intervene (Heinze 2007). Instead, the rhetoric of the Bush administration was adopted instrumentally in response to external pressure. While adopting international human rights discourse that would have afforded US intervention or leadership in intervention on behalf of the international community, the Bush administration did not believe in the validity of the solidarist notion of moral responsibility embedded in the Genocide Convention and had no intention of advancing it. Nor did they intend to support rhetoric with action. Rather, the Secretary of State's remarks before the Senate Foreign Relations Committee downplayed any obligation to intervene, as Secretary Powell (2004) insisted that despite his finding of genocide in Darfur, "no new action is dictated by [such a] determination." Instead, Powell suggested that "the most practical contribution we can make ... is to do everything we can to increase the number of African Union monitors." President Bush likewise downplayed calls for intervention, stating, "we shouldn't be committing troops. We ought to be working with the African Union to do so" (Associated Press 2004).

As pointed out by Heinze (2007), the willingness of the Bush administration to employ the rhetoric of genocide stands as a radical departure from the reasoning that led the Clinton administration to avoid using such language in 1994. While Clinton sought to deny what the international community knew about genocide in Rwanda, Bush continuously branded the situation in Darfur "genocide" despite significant uncertainty on behalf of the international community as to whether this commonplace could be justifiably invoked. Following Powell's determination, no other permanent member of the UN Security Council followed suit. On the contrary, the UN Commission of Inquiry on Darfur, authorized by UN Security Council Resolution 1564, concluded in January of 2005 that "the Government of Sudan has not pursued a policy of genocide." According to Steele (2007), however, unlike his predecessor during the Rwanda genocide, Bush did not perceive the declaration of genocide as conferring an obligation to intervene in Darfur on humanitarian grounds.[6] By concluding that genocide had not taken place, the UN Commission provided the US with an opportunity to deploy the discourse on genocide while appeasing expectations of military intervention. By utilizing rhetorical commonplaces in this way, the Bush administration was thus able to give the impression that they, unlike the Clinton administration a decade earlier, took a firm stance against "crimes against humanity." The practical implication, however, was the employment of the rhetoric of genocide as a substitute for more decisive action.

The north–south conflict and domestic pressure for action

The politics in Congress that led to the use of the rhetoric of genocide in reference to Darfur have their roots in the racial and/or religious undertones of Sudan's "other" civil war – the north–south conflict (discussed below). The Sudan People's Liberation Army (SPLA)/Sudan People's Liberation Movement (SPLM) rebels had been fighting the Islamist government since 1983, defending the predominantly non-Arab and non-Muslim populations in the southern providences (referred to by the media as "Black" or "African" Sudanese) from the government's brutal policies of forced "Islamization" and "Arabization." The elements of religious persecution of Christians and enslavement of "Blacks" made it of particular concern to evangelical and African American constituencies in the United States. Influential members of Congress with strong evangelical bases, including Tom Tancredo (R-CO), Spencer Bachus (R-AL), and Donald Payne (D-MD) in the House, and Sam Brownback (R-KS) and Bill Frist (R-TN) in the Senate, consequently took up what became known as the "faith-based Sudan coalition," bringing about landmark legislation such as the 1998 International Religious Freedom Act and the 2002 Sudan Peace Act. President Bush, also with a strong evangelical base, supported the initiatives of Congress toward ending Sudan's civil war, proclaiming in 2001 that his administration would place religious persecution and atrocities in Sudan at the forefront of his foreign policy agenda (New York Times 2001).

As a result of evangelical zeal for ending the persecution of Christians in the southern part of the country, Sudan already had an attentive constituency in Washington when the crisis in Darfur erupted in 2003. The timing of statements urging action 10 years after Rwanda attracted the attention of Congress, and the concern over the north–south conflict spilled over into a concern over events in Darfur. In August 2004, nearly 50 religious leaders organized by the National Association of Evangelicals, pairing the concept of genocide with the responsibility to protect, called on the president to take "swift action" to stop the genocide in Darfur, including delivering humanitarian aid, considering military options, and working to remove Sudan from the UN Human Rights Commission (Heinze 2007).

Also the African American leadership was influential in putting Darfur at the top of the agenda in US foreign policy circles. The Darfur crisis was widely portrayed in media as "Arab on African" violence, thus transferring to the Darfur crisis an identity frame similar to that which prevailed in the north–south conflict (De Waal 2005). In particular, the issue of enslavement, prevalent in both conflicts, served to draw the African American community into coalition with evangelicals, further contributing to the spillover of concern from the north–south conflict to Darfur (Hertzke 2005). Deploying rhetorical commonplaces affording action in defense of human rights, these pressure groups reproduced the state as a moral actor with a moral responsibility extending beyond the boundary demarcations of the state by characterizing the protection of civilians in Darfur as an activity of the state. In July, members of the Congressional Black Caucus demanded an end to the genocide in Darfur, organizing a protest in front of the Sudanese embassy in Washington, wherein Congressmen Charles Rangel (D-NY), Bobby Rush (D-IL), and Joe Hoeffel (D-PA) were among those arrested by police (Naylor 2004).

Beyond the efforts by the evangelical and African American community, the Congressional declaration of the situation in Darfur as "genocide" (US House and US Senate, 22 July 2004) signaled a public mindset in support of strong American action in Darfur (Kull and Destler 1999). This was consistent with earlier polls indicating widespread support for US action on genocide in general. However, while support for the principle that the US has a moral obligation to suppress genocides and situations of mass atrocities is consistent and firm, the extent to which Americans are willing to back such an "obligation" with concrete action in specific cases is less clear. Research indicates that significant differences exist when it comes to Americans' support for different types of missions, depending on how survey questions are worded. Explicit or implicit referrals to multilateralism (which implies legitimacy); to burden sharing; to whether or not the mission is consensual; and to whether or not US ground troops are to be used, have proven to impact poll results significantly (Kull 2004; Mayroz undated).[7] Due to the ambiguous nature of domestic opinion on these questions related to foreign policy and the specific nature of the concept of US responsibility to act in response to situations of severe human rights violations, policy makers tend to err on the side of caution. This is particularly the case when dealing with situations emerging in highly contested normative spaces, such as those related to whether the sacrifice of American soldiers' lives to protect innocent civilians abroad can be morally justified. Because "no US president has ever suffered politically for his indifference to its occurrence," according to Samantha Power "[n]o US president has ever made genocide prevention a priority" (Power 2003: xxi). Thus, while domestic support for US action in Darfur was strong, it was insufficient to compel the Bush administration to buttress rhetoric with action.

Adding to the government's ability to escape expectations of a more forceful response to the Darfur atrocities despite the deployment of rhetorical commonplaces warranting action, was the lack of media attention devoted to the conflict. Following the declaration of "genocide" by the Bush administration, it took almost a year for media to engage the story. Once they did, a number of factors quickly reduced the frequency and quality of coverage: the salience of Iraq and Afghanistan; the presidential elections; the lack of a significant security or economic angle; foreign-news budgetary constraints; the difficulty of journalists to gain access to the region; and the alleged slowness of Western media in covering mass killings of people of African descent. This was true of most of the print media (Mayroz undated).[8] This low salience of the issue contributed to lowering the expectation that pairing the rhetoric of genocide with a responsibility to protect would be accompanied by more forceful humanitarian action, thus allowing the Bush administration to interpret the state as a moral actor based on a pluralist limited understanding of how far moral responsibility extends in international affairs.

International concerns

In contrast to the widespread domestic support for US action in Darfur generated by the discourse on genocide, the Bush administration's deployment of rhetorical commonplaces was met with widespread skepticism in international circles. While characterized as "Rwanda in slow motion" (Lake and Prendergast 2004), the atrocities in Darfur were qualitatively and quantitatively different from those in Rwanda ten years prior. Thus, when the United States continued to employ the rhetoric of genocide in the context of Darfur even after the UN had released its conclusion that genocide had not taken place, suspicion arose that the US was looking for a pretext to invade another oil-rich and predominantly Arab and Muslim state (Global News Wire 2004a). Not surprisingly, Sudan categorically rejected the US finding, and was quick to suggest that the accusation of genocide could severely complicate not only peace negotiations with the Darfur rebels, but also the Naivasha accords (DaCosta 2004). Likewise, the Arab League took the position that the situation in Darfur was neither genocide nor ethnic cleaning and accused the US administration of "exploit[ing] the situation in Darfur for ... the US election campaign ... to win black votes," a sentiment echoed by officials from Médecins Sans Frontières (BBC 2004). AU officials, realizing that US support was crucial to their efforts to demonstrate the organization's effectiveness in addressing crises in Africa, avoided condemning the US finding, but called on US officials to provide evidence to support their claim (Global News Wire 2004b). Even before the US administration made its position public, the European Union made a statement in response to Congress's genocide resolution, saying that the Darfur crisis did not meet the legal requirements of genocide (Agence France Presse 2004). Especially after the UN Commission of Inquiry released its report on Darfur, the United States thus found itself isolated among its international peers on the issue of genocide (Heinze 2007). *The Observer* (2004) consequently accused the United States of "hyping" genocide in Darfur.

The prevailing political realities at the time fuelled further skepticism. In a context in which Western media regularly identify Arabs as the instigators of terrorism, the invocation of the term "genocide" and the framing of the crisis as "Arab on African" was viewed as yet another selective and unfair vilification of Arabs as "genocidaires" (De Waal 2005). In light of the war in Iraq, former Assistant Secretary-General of the UN, Ramesh Thakur (Economist 2004: 11), thus openly disparaged Western "humanitarians clamoring for another war," arguing that "Western intervention in Darfur would be exploited as yet another assault on Arabs and Muslims." This stemmed from the view that, in the case of Iraq, "most actors in international and world society believed that humanitarian justifications were used to mask the exercise of hegemonic power" (Williams and Bellamy 2005: 36–37; Slim 2004: 811–828). As Human Rights Watch's Michael Clough (2005: 8) put it, "the fact that the Bush administration was waging a globally unpopular war in Iraq without a UN mandate inevitably affected how other UN member states responded [to the US's genocide finding], particularly once the graphic images of ... Abu Ghraib were broadcast around the world."

The expanded notion of moral responsibility enshrined in the R2P thus arguably suffered a legitimacy blow after the US attempt to justify

Western intervention in Iraq as primarily "humanitarian." Some developing countries likened the R2P to a "Trojan horse" for big-power meddling (Bellamy 2005), while others were wary of becoming potential targets for intervention (Steinberg, cited in Hoge 2008; Williams and Bellamy 2005: 36–40). With the US military already spread thin in Iraq and Afghanistan, therefore, many administration officials were relieved when the UN Commission announced that there was not enough evidence to suggest that genocide was unfolding in Darfur. Ironically, it was the lack of US credibility abroad and fear of the Jacksonian Bush administration's exploitative motives that provided political cover for the US government's non-intervention following its own deployment of rhetorical conclusion of genocide in Darfur (Heinze 2007). Beyond this skepticism toward the Jacksonian instrumental and erratic foreign policy of the US government, other geo-strategic factors significantly impacted the response to Darfur.

Geo-strategic issues played a significant role in generating international hesitation to condemn Sudan by accusing its government of genocide in Darfur. Despite its tough rhetoric, the United States' interest in oil and intelligence-exchange shaped its preference to keep the Sudanese government on its good side in the "war on terror" (Williams and Bellamy 2005: 36–40). These and concerns of anti-Western terrorist activities arguably trumped concerns over human rights abuses on the ground. Also Russia and China wanted to protect their lucrative oil interests and arms trade with Sudan, threatening to veto any forceful UN Security Council action (Goodman 2004; McDoom 2005; Steele 2007; Badescu and Bergholm 2009).[9] Most importantly, the considerable diplomatic and financial investments by Western states and the Intergovernmental Authority on Development (IGAD) in the mediation of the north–south conflict in Sudan hindered involvement in Darfur.

The Machakos–Naivasha Agreement was a diplomatic effort coordinated through the IGAD and intended to resolve the conflict between the SPLA/SPLM and the Government of Sudan (GoS). It resulted in the signing of the Comprehensive Peace Agreement (CPA) in January 2005. The CPA was envisioned to end the Second Sudanese Civil War, develop democratic governance countrywide, share oil revenues, and hold a referendum on southern secession in 2011. While attempts were made to treat the north–south conflict as separate to the Darfur conflict, the UN Secretary-General's Special Representative for Internally Displaced Persons, Francis Deng (UN Economic and Social Council 2005), suggested that the conflicts were inextricably linked. He warned that deploying protection forces to Darfur under Chapter VII of the UN

Charter would provoke armed resistance by Khartoum, "turn Darfur into a theatre for another layer of conflict," and "fundamentally undermine the [Naivasha] peace process and lead it to collapse and plunge the whole country into an even greater crisis."

Accordingly, throughout 2004, the Western members of the IGAD Partners Forum chose to prioritize the diplomatic struggle to end the SPLA/SPLM–GoS war over addressing the conflict in Darfur. This was done, at least in part, on the grounds that while the war in Darfur was tragic and had left many thousands of people dead, the war in the south had raged for over two decades, killing millions. In this view, peace in Sudan was to be built by first fixing the north–south axis, and later resolving the peripheral conflicts in the west and east of the country. Several analysts supported the argument that the best chance of securing a political solution to Darfur was through implementation of the Naivasha Accords, which involved a power-sharing deal that would allow the late SPLA/SPLM leader, John Garang, to serve as Vice President in Khartoum to President Bashir (Slim 2004). Mukesh Kapila, the United Nations Resident Coordinator for the Sudan in 2003–2004, recalls the response in New York to the crisis in Darfur: "The reaction in the political parts of the Secretariat was that yes, they knew that Darfur was terrible, but they had to wait for the north–south conflict to be solved, and then Darfur would also be solved" (cited in Lebor 2006: 155c). The situation has striking similarities to both Bosnia and Rwanda. Kapila continues (*ibid.*):

> Except for OCHA [the Office for the Coordination of Humanitarian Affairs], the humanitarian affairs department, there was no appetite for understanding the gravity of the situation, that this was a worsening trend and that we needed to do something about it. There is a parallel with Bosnia here. This was more than a lack of energy or lack of will. There was a fundamental feeling among very senior people that this was a very inconvenient development and they would rather not know about it. It did not fit the United Nations' paradigm for Sudan, of a smooth peace agreement and a new order. Real-life facts were somewhat inconvenient.

Backed by Jan Egeland, United Nations Undersecretary-General for Humanitarian Affairs and Emergency Relief, Mukesh Kapila traveled to visit members of the Security Council: "Almost everywhere I went I was told not to make too much noise, because of the north–south accords. Washington said that they did want to take Darfur to the

Security Council, but London would not agree, and [the US] would not do anything without London's agreement" (Kapila cited in Lebor 2006: 161). In the view and interest of these actors, the Machakos–Naivasha peace process had to be concluded before any other Sudanese problems could be addressed (Williams and Bellamy 2005: 36–40).

In addition to providing international political cover for inaction, returning the focus back to the stalled north–south negotiations in November 2004 enabled the US administration to deflect calls for more decisive action in Darfur by US constituencies. The United States had invested considerable diplomatic capital in the Naivasha process and was eager to see it implemented, as were many in the faith-based Sudan coalition. Ending the north–south conflict was, after all, the original promise of President Bush to his evangelical base, so it made political sense to not let the Darfur crisis spoil the entire process, especially in an election year. Thus, when important domestic constituencies put pressure on the administration over Darfur, the administration was effectively able to deflect such calls by raising the possibility that intervening or otherwise confronting Khartoum would jeopardize the very goal that these constituencies were fighting for in the first place: an end to the north–south conflict and the religious persecution that accompanied it (Heinze 2007).

This concern over the success of the Naivasha process in both domestic and international circles, in tandem with general international trepidation about American interventionism as a result of the Iraq war, thus contributed to a political atmosphere wherein US officials could pair rhetorical commonplaces affording forceful military action without generating an expectation of intervention. While the degree of legitimacy possessed by the United States as a global enforcer of human rights during the 1990s would have facilitated international demands for the US to intervene in Rwanda, therefore, it was the precise lack of legitimacy that contributed to the absence of pressure on the US to act in response to the atrocities in Darfur.

Implications for the state as a moral actor

Already during his campaign, Bush was clear about his priorities and preferred approach in response to situations of severe human rights violations:

> Africa's important. And we've got to do a lot of work in Africa to promote democracy and trade. It's an important continent. But

there's got to be priorities. And the Middle East is a priority for a lot of reasons as is Europe and the Far East, and our own hemisphere. Those are my four top priorities should I be the president. It's not to say we won't be engaged [in Africa], and working hard to get other nations to come together to prevent atrocity [like in Rwanda]. I thought the best example of handling a [genocide] situation was East Timor when we provided logistical support to the Australians; support that only we can provide. I thought that was a good model. But we can't be all things to all people in the world. I am worried about over-committing our military around the world. I want to be judicious in its use. I don't think nation-building missions are worthwhile.

(PBS 2000)

Although several aspects of the president's approach to foreign policy changed in the aftermath of 9/11 – and also, the president himself came to champion concerted action against AIDS and malaria in Africa – this original, reluctant approach with regard to engagement in Africa was arguably reflected in Darfur, where the Bush administration succeeded in achieving two seemingly contradictory goals: avoiding engagement in a conflict posing little threat to narrowly defined national interests while containing the political costs and avoiding the moral stigma associated with standing by while genocide unfolds (Power 2003: 508; 2002: 85–95). Appearing as if they were complying with the Genocide Convention and the R2P doctrine by deploying rhetorical commonplaces reflective of a solidarist expanded notion of moral responsibility in international relations, the US government did little of what this notion actually prescribes. On the contrary, the Bush administration pursued a consciously ineffective line of action, deploying the discourse on genocide instrumentally. By referencing a solidarist expanded notion of moral responsibility to promote narrowly defined national interests, the Jacksonian Bush administration reinforced its pluralist view of the state as a moral actor and its accompanying limited notion of moral responsibility in international relations.[10]

The case of Darfur thus seems to indicate that the solidarist principles embedded in the Genocide Convention and the R2P weakened during the time of the Bush administration. One must wonder to what extent the United States would have reacted to Darfur at all had it not already been paying close attention to the events concerning Sudan's "other civil war." Yet, while the Bush administration's instrumental adaptation of the R2P may be considered to undermine and even regress the solidarist expanded notion of moral responsibility during this specific set of debates, Mr. Bush's misrepresentation ironically also highlights its importance. Accepted as an international doctrine by the UN at the 2005 World Summit, the international community had considerable incentive to appear to be taking action in accordance with the R2P in response to the Darfur atrocities. This incentive was exacerbated by pressure exerted by domestic pressure groups, NGOs, demonstrators around the world, and pleas for action by celebrities including George Clooney and Angelina Jolie (New York Times 2006). In response to these pressures, the Bush administration's acknowledgement of the overall validity of the notion that there exists an international responsibility to protect reflected in the rhetorical commonplaces deployed in the circumstances of Darfur impacted its advancement. If the US considered the concept of the state as a moral actor and the accompanying notion of moral responsibility enshrined in the R2P to be without value, they would not have invoked these rhetorical commonplaces to promote expectations of accompanying action. As Ramesh Thakur suggests (2010): "normative imitation is the most sincere form of flattery." The Bush administration's response to Darfur, although not reflected in action, thus arguably proves the very existence of an international responsibility to protect across political and cultural boundaries.

Moreover, as pointed out by Risse, Ropp, and Sikkink (1999), while governments may initially invoke a discourse reflecting a more expanded notion of moral responsibility with the purpose of furthering their instrumentally defined interests, the more they justify their interests, the more others will start challenging their arguments and the validity claims inherent in them. According to this line of reasoning, the incongruence between words and actions portrayed by the Bush administration could potentially generate pressure for coherence that, with time, will generate more consistent and coherent responses to situations of severe human rights violations, thus shaping the state as a moral actor based on an expanded notion of moral responsibility in international affairs.

Notes

1   The R2P confirms that "state sovereignty" does not exist without limits by strengthening the foundation for collective responses to situations of genocide, war crimes, ethnic cleansing, and crimes against humanity (ICISS 2001). The R2P advocates a reconsideration of sovereignty to include a dual responsibility: "externally – to respect the sovereignty of other states, and internally, to respect the dignity and basic rights of all people within

the state" (*ibid.*: 8, §1.35). According to the report, commissioned by the Government of Canada, a state must bear "the primary responsibility for the protection of its peoples." Moreover, should a state fail in this responsibility; either independently or in partnership with external actors, then "the principle of non-intervention yields to the international responsibility to protect" (*ibid.*: xi). This report thus asserts the notion of "conditional sovereignty," and a shift in the foundation of international dialogue from that of a "right to intervene" to a "responsibility to protect" a population within a state's care.

2   Estimates for the pre-conflict population of Darfur range from about 4 million to close to 7 million. Experts have noted uncertainty regarding the population estimate for Darfur due to the lack of a current census and the fact that migration in this region occurs even during non-conflict times (Badescu and Bergholm 2009).

3   According to confidential interviews, close to 75 percent of the entire AU budget is paid by South Africa, Egypt, Libya, Nigeria, and Algeria alone (Badescu and Bergholm 2009).

4   According to a State official, the key factor in the US government's genocide determination was the intent of the Sudanese government regarding its actions in Darfur – its intent to destroy, in whole or in part, a specific group of people. The number of deaths attributable to the crisis was not a critical factor (Mayroz 2008).

5   The N'Djamena Agreement, signed between the Sudanese government and Darfurian rebels in Chad on 8 April.

6   Article I of the Genocide Convention reads, "the Contracting Parties confirm that genocide ... is a crime under international law which they undertake to prevent and to punish." Article VIII of the treaty further suggests that states "may call upon the competent organs of the United Nations to take such action ... as they consider appropriate for the prevention and suppression of acts of genocide." Original and secondary sources on the Genocide Convention now suggest that President Bush's interpretation of the Convention was in accordance with the negotiators of the Draft Convention, whose objective on the matter of prevention and punishment was to debate whether and the extent to which "states [should] provide for the prevention and punishment [of genocide] in their national legislatures," and not necessarily to confer an obligation to intervene militarily. For further discussion, see Heinze (2007, 2004).

7   Overall, a majority believes that promoting human rights is an important priority for US foreign policy. The sharp drop in support of human rights at the end of the 1990s and beginning of the second Bush administration returned to the average level of previous decades during the early 2000s. In July 2004, principled support among both policymakers and the mass public for using US military forces to suppress genocide was high. Moreover, despite significant differences, this stance applied to unilateral as well as multilateral action. According to one poll, 70 percent of the American public and 73 percent of surveyed political elites believed that states should have the right to use military force to prevent severe human rights violations, even without UN approval (Chicago Council on Foreign Relations 2004). Further, 94 percent of American leaders and 85 percent of

the public said that the UN Security Council should have the right to authorize the use of military force to prevent severe human rights violations (*ibid.*). Initially, principled support even existed for the use of US troops to intervene to stop genocide. In 2004, 75 percent of the public and 86 percent of American leaders favored the deployment of US troops to stop a government from committing genocide (*ibid.*: 29; Mayroz undated). However, an ICG and Zogbi International poll conducted a year later (ICG and Zogbi International 2005) showed a marked difference to the strong principled support in 2004. Majority support for multilateral or even unilateral action without using American troops was less high but still existed. Support for sending marines to Darfur was as low as 38 percent. A third poll from June 2005 indicated increased support (54%) of US troop deployment as part of a multilateral force (Program on International Policy Attitudes 2005). Despite this increase, these polls suggest decreased support for humanitarian intervention when compared with public opinion ten years earlier. In July 1994, support for multilateral troop deployment in Bosnia and Rwanda was 62 percent. However, when asked how this support would have been affected had the UN declared "genocide" in these crises, 80 percent in both cases supported multilateral and American military response (Kull 2004: 6).

8   According to the 2006 Carma report on Western media coverage of humanitarian disasters, the crisis in Darfur generated a total of 312 articles in 2004 and 2005. Comparatively, this number was appallingly low. The first calendar year featured only two articles in *The Guardian,* while a combined total of 165 words dealt with Darfur in news in brief segments in *The Independent* (Gabriel 2009). In the *New York Times,* only one story was run in 2003. In 2004, 125 stories were run, while 58 stories were published in 2005 and 43 were run from 1 January through 16 May 2006 (Zagorski 2008).

9   It is worth noting here that while in the case of Darfur, the looming threat of the permanent members of the Security Council utilizing their veto power resulted in inaction, the threat to veto has in other cases encouraged intervention without Security Council authorization. This was reflected in NATO's failure to seek Security Council authorization for its bombing campaign against Yugoslavia in 1999 and the US's decision to intervene in Iraq despite the lack of Security Council authorization in 2003. Unauthorized interventions signal a disturbing trend among the Western powers to avoid compliance with the UN Charter when humanitarian imperatives and political considerations seem compelling to them, casting serious doubt on the interest of the Western powers to vigorously pursue the type of institutional reforms in the UN, including limitation to the veto, necessary to allow the UN to fulfill its moral responsibilities consistently and coherently when faced with situations of grave human rights violations (Lepard 2002).

10   By highlighting the instrumental adaptation of rhetoric in order to advance narrowly defined national interests in the case of Darfur, I do not intend to undermine other aspects of the administration's neo-conservative and broadly interventionist rhetoric that were based on a rights-oriented attitude toward democracy. In particular, elements related to the president's own

interest in the fight against AIDS and malaria in Africa suggest a more soli-darist understanding of world politics and an expanded notion of US moral responsibility, linked to a certain extent to a notion of Christian charity (Bush 2010).

References

Agence France Presse (2004) US Senate Leader Insists "Genocide" Underway in Darfur, Despite EU Statement. 10 August. Available at http://reliefweb.int/report/sudan/us-senate-leader-insists-genocide-underway-darfur-despite-eu-statement (accessed 19 January 2015).

Allen, M. (2000) Bush's Gaffes are Back as Debates Near. *Washington Post*, 1 October: A8.

Associated Press (2004) Bush and Kerry on the Issue of Sudan. Associated Press, 28 October. Available at www.sudantribune.com/spip.php?article6208 (accessed 19 January 2015).

Bacevich, A. (2008) *The Limits of Power: The End of American Exceptionalism.* New York: Metropolitan Books.

Badescu, C.G. and Bergholm, L. (2009) The Responsibility to Protect and the Conflict in Darfur: The Big Let-Down. *Security Dialogue* 40: 287–309.

Barker, A. (2004) Bush Faces Pressure on Sudan Genocide. Financial Times, July 14. Available at www.ft.com/cms/s/0/f86e1286-d532-11d8-8f7c-00000e2511c8.html#axzz3OntePQJN (accessed 19 January 2015).

BBC (2004) Sudan News Agency on MSFs "Categorical Rejection" of Powell's Darfur Remarks. BBC News, 13 September.

Bellamy, A. (2005) Responsibility to Protect or Trojan Horse? The Crisis in Darfur and Humanitarian Intervention After Iraq. *Ethics and International Affairs* 19(2): 31–53.

Bush, G.W. (2010) *Decision Points.* New York: Crown.

—— (2007) *The United States Response to the Darfur Crisis.* 19 September. Washington, DC: Bureau of Public Affairs. Available at www.archive.usun.state.gov/fact_sheet/ps_w5.pdf (accessed 5 June 2010).

—— (2006) President Participates in Discussion on the Global War on Terror. 11 January. Available at www.whitehouse.gov/news/releases/2006/01/20060111-7.html (accessed 3 October 2010).

—— (2004a) State of the Union Address. 20 January. Available at http://whitehouse.georgewbush.org/news/2004/012004-SOTU.asp (accessed 3 May 2011).

—— (2004b) Graduation Speech at the US Air Force Academy. June. Available at www.whitehouse.gov/briefing-room/ (accessed 8 April 2010).

—— (2004c) Bush Proposes Democracy Fund: President Bush's Address to the 59th UN General Assembly. 21 September. Available at http://iipdigital.usembassy.gov/st/english/texttrans/2004/09/20040921124122eaifas0.2810633.html#axzz3Os7g5xPH (accessed 19 January 2015).

—— (2000) Presidential Debate on Foreign Policy, Wake Forest University,

Winston-Salem, NC. 11 October. Available at www.ontheissues.org/Archive/
Wake_Forest_debate_Foreign_Policy.htm (accessed 8 September 2010).

Chicago Council on Foreign Relations (2004) *Global Views 2004: American
Public Opinion and Foreign Policy.* Chicago, IL: Chicago Council on
Foreign Relations. Available at www.thechicagocouncil.org/UserFiles/File/
POS_Topline%20Reports/POS%202004/US%20Public%20Opinion%20
Global_Views_2004_US.pdf (accessed 15 February 2010).

Clough, M. (2005) *Darfur: Whose Responsibility to Protect?* New York: Human
Rights Watch. Available at www.hrw.org/legacy/wr2k5/darfur/darfur.pdf
(accessed 13 January 2015).

Daalder, Ivo H., and James M. Lindsay (2003) *America Unbound.* Washington,
DC: Brookings Institution.

DaCosta, G. (2004) Sudan Says UN Genocide Declaration for Darfur Could
Hurt Peace Talks. Associated Press, 10 September.

Dale, H. (2008) Bush's Foreign Policy. *The Washington Times*, 28 October.
Available at www.washingtontimes.com/news/2008/oct/29/bushs-foreign-
policy (accessed 1 May 2011).

De Waal, A. (2005) Who are the Darfurians? Arab and African Identities,
Violence and External Engagement. *African Affairs* 104(415): 181–205.

Economist (2004) Sudan Can't Wait. *The Economist*, 29 July. Available at
www.economist.com/node/2963177 (accessed 19 January 2015).

Fessenden, H. (2004a) The Semantics of "Genocide" and How it Pertains to
Sudan. *CQ Weekly* 62: 1639.

—— (2004b) Lawmakers Seek Viable Solutions to Sudan's Humanitarian
Crisis. *CQ Weekly* 62: 1638–1639.

Gabriel, G. (2009) *Study: Darfur in the Media – From Crisis to Context.*
Available at http://martinfrost.ws/htmlfiles/may2009/darfur-in-the-media.pdf
(accessed 25 August 2014).

Global News Wire (2004a) Sudan Prefers AU Mediation in Darfur Crisis. Asia
Africa Intelligence Wire, 12 September.

—— (2004b) AU Official Asks USA to Provide Evidence of Genocide in
Darfur. 13 September.

Goodman, P.S. (2004) China Invests Heavily in Sudan's Oil Industry. *The
Washington Post*, 23 December: A01.

Heinze, E. (2007) The Rhetoric of Genocide in US Foreign Policy: Rwanda and
Darfur Compared. *Political Science Quarterly* 122(3): 359–383.

—— (2004) Law, Force, and Human Rights: The Search for a Sufficiently
Principled Legal Basis for Humanitarian Intervention. *Journal of Conflict
Studies* 24: 5–32.

Hertzke, A.D. (2005) The Shame of Darfur. *First Things* 156: 16–22.

Hoge, W. (2008) Intervention, Hailed as a Concept, But Shunned in Practice. *New
York Times*, 8 January. Available at www.nytimes.com/2008/01/20/world/
africa/20nations.html?pagewanted=all&_r=0 (accessed 19 January 2015).

Human Rights Watch (2004) *Darfur in Flames: Atrocities in Western Sudan.*
New York: Human Rights Watch.

ICISS (2001) *The Responsibility to Protect: Report of the International Commission on Intervention and State Sovereignty.* December. Ottawa: The International Development Research Centre. Available at http://responsibilitytoprotect.org/ICISSReport.pdf (accessed 13 January 2015).

International Crisis Group (2007) *Darfur's New Security Reality.* Africa Report 134. Nairobi: International Crisis Group.

International Peace Academy (2007) *The AU in Sudan: Lessons for the African Standby Force.* New York: International Peace Academy.

Kagan, R. (2008) Neocon Nation: Neoconservatism, c. 1776. *World Affairs,* spring. Available at www.worldaffairsjournal.org/index.php?q=article/neocon-nation-neoconservatism-c-1776 (accessed 3 November 2010).

Kapila, M. (2004) West Sudan's Darfur Conflict "World's Greatest Humanitarian Crisis." *Sudan Tribune,* 19 March. Available at www.sudantribune.com/West-Sudan-s-Darfur-conflict-world,2161 (accessed 7 September 2010).

Kaufman, R. (2007) *In Defense of the Bush Doctrine.* Lexington, KY: University Press of Kentucky.

Kristof, N.D. (2004) Will We Say "Never Again" Yet Again? *The New York Times,* 27 March. Available at www.nytimes.com/2004/03/27/opinion/will-we-say-never-again-yet-again.html (accessed 19 January 2015).

Kull, S. (2004) *Americans on the Crisis in Sudan.* Washington, DC: Program on International Policy Attitudes (PIPA). Available at www.pipa.org/OnlineReports/Africa/Sudan_Jul04/Sudan_Jul04_rpt.pdf (accessed 3 March 2010).

Kull, S. and Destler, M.I. (1999) *Misreading the Public: The Myth of a New Isolationism.* Washington DC: Brookings Institution Press.

Lake, A. and Prendergast, J. (2004) Stopping Sudan's Slow-Motion Genocide. *Boston Globe,* 20 May. Available at www.enoughproject.org/news/stopping-sudans-slow-motion-genocide-boston-globe (accessed 19 January 2015).

Lebor, A. (2006) *Complicity with Evil: The United Nations in the Age of Modern Genocide.* Harrisburg, VA: R.R. Donnelley.

Lepard, B. (2002) *Rethinking Humanitarian Intervention: A Fresh Approach based on Fundamental Ethical Principles in International Law and World Religions.* University Park, PA: Pennsylvania State University Press.

MacAskill, E. (2004) Stakes Rise as US Declares Darfur Killings Genocide. *The Guardian,* 10 September. Available at www.guardian.co.uk/politics/2004/sep/10/1 (accessed 13 January 2015).

Mayroz, E. (2008) Ever Again? The United States, genocide suppression, and the crisis in Darfur. *Journal of Genocide Research* 10(3): 359–388.

—— (undated) US Policy on Darfur and the Moral Obligation to Suppress. Available at www.gpanet.org/content/us-policy-darfur-and-moral-obligation-suppress (accessed 2 April 2011).

McDoom, O. (2005) China's Interests in Sudan Bring Diplomatic Cover. Reuters, 2 December. Available at www.sudantribune.com/spip.php?page=imprimable&id_article=13090 (accessed 19 January 2015).

Mead, W.R. (2002) *Special Providence*. New York: Routledge.

Morgenthau, H. (1948) *Politics Among Nations*. New York: Alfred A. Knopf.

Natsios, A.S. (2008) Beyond Darfur: Sudan's Slide Toward Civil War. *Council on Foreign Relations* 87(3): 77–93.

Naylor, B. (2004) Lawmakers Arrested at Sudan Protest. National public radio broadcast. *All Things Considered*, 25 July.

New York Times (2006) Demonstrations Around the World Draw Attention to Darfur Crisis. *New York Times*, 18 September. Available at www.nytimes.com/2006/09/18/world/africa/18sudan.html?fta=y (accessed 19 January 2015).

—— (2001) Bush Condemns Suppression of Religious Freedom in Sudan. *New York Times*, 4 May. www.nytimes.com/2001/05/04/world/bush-condemns-suppression-of-religious-freedom-in-sudan.html (accessed 19 January 2015).

Observer (2004) US "Hyping" Darfur Genocide Fear. *The Observer*, 3 October. Available at www.theguardian.com/world/2004/oct/03/usa.sudan (accessed 19 January 2015).

Owens, M.T. (2009) The Bush Doctrine: The Foreign Policy of Republican Empire. Available at www.fpri.org/orbis/5301/owens.bushdoctrine.pdf (accessed 3 December 2010).

—— (2006) America's Role in the World: Republican Empire and the Bush Doctrine. Available at www.ashbrook.org/publicat/oped/owens/06/americasrole.html (accessed 23 August 2010).

PBS (2000) Presidential Debate. 12 October. Available at www.pbs.org/newshour/bb/politics/july-dec00/for-policy_10-12.html (accessed 1 May 2011).

Penketh, A. (2005) White House Described Darfur as "Genocide" to Please Christian Right. *The Independent*, 2 July. Available at www.independent.co.uk/news/world/africa/white-house-described-darfur-as-genocide-to-please-christian-right-296269.html (accessed 19 January 2015).

Powell, C.L. (2004) Written Remarks of Secretary of State to Senate Foreign Relations Committee on the Crisis in Darfur. Available at www.whitehouse.gov/interactive/sudan_gen.html (accessed 9 September).

Power, S. (2004) Testimony of Samantha Power. Committee on House International Relations Subcommittee on Africa, 108th Congress, 2nd session.

—— (2003) *A Problem from Hell: America in the Age of Genocide*. New York: Harper Perennial.

—— (2002) Raising the Cost of Genocide. *Dissent* 49(2): 85–95.

—— (2001) Bystanders to Genocide: Why the United States Let the Rwandan Tragedy Happen. *The Atlantic Monthly*, September. Available at www.theatlantic.com/magazine/archive/2001/09/bystanders-to-genocide/304571 (accessed 19 January 2015).

Prendergast, J. (2004) Sudan's Ravines of Death. *The New York Times*, 15 July.

Available at www.nytimes.com/2004/07/15/opinion/sudan-s-ravines-of-death.html (accessed 19 January 2015).

Program on International Policy Attitudes (2005) *The Darfur Crisis: African and American Public Opinion.* June. Washington, DC: Program on International Policy Attitudes (PIPA). Available at www.globescan.com/news_archives/GS_PIPA_darfur_report.pdf (accessed 22 January 2010).

Prunier, G. (2007) *Darfur: The Ambiguous Genocide?*, 2nd edn. Ithaca, NY: Cornell University Press.

Reeves, E. (2004) Unnoticed Genocide. *Washington Post*, 25 February. Available at http://sudanreeves.org/2014/01/07/unnoticed-genocide-the-washington-post-february-25-2004 (accessed 19 January 2015).

Rice, S. (2005) Why Darfur Can't be Left to Africa. *Washington Post*, 7 August. Available at www.washingtonpost.com/wp-dyn/content/article/2005/08/05/AR2005080501988.html (accessed 19 January 2015).

Risse, T., Ropp, S.C. and Sikkink, K. (eds.) (1999) *The Power of Human Rights: International Norms and Domestic Change.* Cambridge: Cambridge University Press.

Shurkin, M. (2005) France and the Darfur Crisis. January. Available at www.brookings.edu/articles/2005/01france_shurkin.aspx (accessed 3 July 2009).

Slim, H. (2004) Dithering over Darfur? A Preliminary Review of the International Response. *International Affairs* 80: 811–828.

Steele, B. J. (2007) Making Words Matter. *International Studies Quarterly* 51: 901–925.

Thakur, R. (2010) The Responsibility to Protect: A Forward Looking Agenda. In W. Kemp, V. Popovski and R. Thakur (eds.), *The Responsibility to Protect and the Problem of the "Kin State"*, 10–27. Tokyo: UN University Press.

UN (2004) "Risk of Genocide Remains Frighteningly Real", Secretary-General Tells Human Rights Commission as He Launches Action Plan to Prevent Genocide. Press release SG/SM/9245. 4 July. Available at www.un.org/News/Press/docs/2004/sgsm9245.doc.htm (accessed 22 August 2010).

—— (1951) Convention on the Prevention and Punishment of the Crime of Genocide. Adopted by Resolution 260 (III) of the UN General Assembly, 9 December 1948. UN Treaty Series no. 1021, 78(277). Available at www.preventgenocide.org/law/convention/text.htm (accessed 6 September 2009).

UN Commission of Inquiry on Darfur (2005) *Report of the International Commission of Inquiry on Darfur to the United Nations Secretary-General.* 25 January. Available at www.un.org/News/dh/sudan/com_inq_darfur.pdf (accessed 17 November 17 2010).

UN Economic and Social Council (2005) Report of the Representative of the Secretary-General on Internally Displaced Persons: Mission to Sudan – the Darfur Crisis. UN doc. E/CN.4/2005/8, 27 September. Available at http://daccess-ods.un.org/TMP/3729404.21104431.html (accessed 13 January 2015).

UN Secretary-General (2004) Action Plan to Prevent Genocide. Speech delivered at the UN Human Rights Commission. 7 April. Press release SG/SM/9197, AFR/893, HR/CN/1077. New York: United Nations.

UN Security Council (2007) Resolution 1564. UN doc. S/RES/1769] (18 September). Available at http://daccess-dds-ny.un.org/doc/UNDOC/GEN/N07/445/52/PDF/N0744552.pdf?OpenElement (accessed 10 January 2010).

—— (2006a) Security Council Expands Mandate of UN Mission in Sudan to Include Darfur. UN doc. S/RES/8821/2006. Available at www.un.org/News/Press/docs/2006/sc8821.doc.htm (10 January 2011).

—— (2006b) Security Council Resolution. UN doc. S/RES/1674/2006. Available at http://daccessdds.un.org/doc/UNDOC/GEN/N06/331/99/PDF/N0633199.pdf?OpenElement (accessed 12 November 2008).

—— (2004a) UN Resolution on Darfur. UN doc. SC/8160. 30 July. Available at: www.un.org/News/Press/docs/2004/sc8160.doc.htm (accessed 16 November 2010).

—— (2004b) Resolution 1564. UN doc. S/RES/1564. 18 September. Available at http://daccess-dds-ny.un.org/doc/UNDOC/GEN/N04/515/47/PDF/N0451547.pdf?OpenElement (accessed 16 November 2010).

US House (2004) Declaring Genocide in Darfur, Sudan. 108th Congress, 2nd session. H. Con. Res.467. Library of US Congress, 22 July.

US Senate (2004) A Concurrent Resolution Declaring Genocide in Darfur, Sudan. S. Con. Res. 133. Library of US Congress, July 22.

Voice of America (2007) Observers Slam US Response to Darfur. 12 April. Available at www.voanews.com/english/news/a-13-Observers-Slam-US-Response-to-Darfur-66712317.html (accessed 13 September 2010).

Washington Post (2006) Bush Signs Law Setting Sanctions on Darfur Crimes. *Washington Post*, 13 October. Available at www.sudantribune.com/spip.php?article18123 (accessed 19 January 2015).

—— (2004) "Realism" and Darfur. *Washington Post*, 1 August. Available at www.washingtonpost.com/wp-dyn/articles/A31077-2004Jul31.html (accessed 19 January 2015).

White House (2002) *The National Security Strategy of the United States of America*. 20 September. Washington, DC: The White House. Available at www.globalsecurity.org/military/library/policy/national/nss-020920.pdf (accessed 7 June 2010).

Williams, P. (2006) Military Responses to Mass Killing: The African Union Mission in Sudan. *International Peacekeeping* 13(2): 168–183.

Williams, P. and Bellamy, A. (2005) The Responsibility To Protect and the Crisis in Darfur. *Security Dialogue* 36(1): 27–47.

Wilson, G. (2006) Darfur Horror Stories Leave Cameron Shaken. *The Telegraph*, 22 November. Available at www.telegraph.co.uk/news/worldnews/1534889/Darfur-horror-stories-leave-Cameron-shaken.html (accessed 2 May 2011).

Zagorski, K. (2008) A Tale of Two Conflicts: Rwanda, Darfur and Media Coverage of Genocide. Paper presented at the annual meeting of the MPSA

Annual National Conference, Palmer House Hotel, Chicago, IL. Available at http://citation.allacademic.com/meta/p266656_index.html   (25   August 2014).

4   The US response to Libya

Now, here is why this matters to us. Left unchecked, we have every reason to believe that Gaddafi would commit atrocities against his people. Many thousands could die. A humanitarian crisis would ensue. The entire region could be destabilized, endangering many of our allies and partners. The calls of the Libyan people for help would go unanswered. The democratic values that we stand for would be overrun. Moreover, the words of the international community would be rendered hollow.

(Barack Obama 2011b)

The 2011 Libyan civil war was an armed conflict between the Transitional National Council coalition, seeking to depose long-standing dictator Muammar Gaddafi, and pro-Gaddafi forces. Provoked by the unrest in Tunisia and Egypt, the initial call for peaceful demonstrations against Gaddafi in February 2011 escalated into open revolts when authorities started arresting human rights campaigners. Gaddafi responded by declaring that he would show "no mercy and no pity" in crushing the rebellion. Within the first six weeks of the civil war, several thousand people were killed and more than 335,600 displaced (UN 2011a). After an initial period of doubt among NATO members as to whether imposing a no-fly zone or otherwise defending civilians in danger was feasible, the UN response was remarkably swift, progressing the responsibility to protect (R2P) from "words to deeds" (Ban ki-Moon) in Security Council Resolution 1970. President Obama justified the US-led military intervention by arguing that it was in "the national interest" of the United States to stop a potential massacre that would have "stained the conscience of the world." However, despite this seemingly promising international response, the nature of, and moral justifications for, the US leadership behind these efforts reveals an administration struggling to reconcile its pluralist and solidarist commitments.

Drawing on the ideological reservoir of the Jeffersonian foreign policy tradition, the Obama administration justified its response to Libya by pairing rhetorical commonplaces affording action on humanitarian grounds with narrowly defined national interests, while simultaneously unpacking the concept of "the national interest" to avoid expectations of more consistent and coherent responses to situations of severe human rights violations in the future. At the same time – and substantiating the Bush rhetoric during Darfur – Obama underscored that there exists a moral responsibility to act, but encouraged others to effectuate the obligation.

The Libya case illustrates how the deployment of certain concepts during a specific set of debates contributed to justifying the continuation of inconsistent responses to situations of mass atrocities, despite the US government's commitment to "never again" stand idly by while genocide unfolds. In this sense, the process of legitimation reinforced the identity of the state as a pluralist moral actor and its accompanying limited notion of moral responsibility in international relations. Yet, by emphasizing the existence of a "responsibility to protect" and the importance of burden-sharing in executing this obligation, this relational constructivist analysis also reveals an administration advancing, however slightly, a solidarist commitment to an expanded notion of moral responsibility within the constraints of a pluralist world.

The Obama Doctrine: a Jeffersonian approach to international burden-sharing

The end of an empire and Obama's Jeffersonian turn

In the realm of foreign policy, Obama has largely been considered a soft-hearted idealist who thinks that he can charm America's enemies. Yet, as Fareed Zakaria suggests (2008), Obama's foreign policy is closer to traditional realism than to liberalism. Drawing on the Jeffersonian tradition in foreign policy, President Obama's first formal National Security Strategy (White House 2010) describes an era in which the United States will have to learn to live within its limits. According to this report, the wars in Iraq and Afghanistan cannot be sustained for much longer and emerging powers like China and Russia will inevitably begin to erode elements of American influence around the globe. Confident in this reality, President Obama suggests that after nearly a decade of organizing its national security policy around counter-terrorism, the United States must now return to a broader agenda. "The burdens of a young century cannot fall on American shoulders alone," Obama says in the introduction of the strategy document. "Indeed, our adversaries would like to see America sap our strength by overextending our power" (*ibid.*: ii).

Assuming that the US can most effectively promote democracy and peace by becoming examples of democracy at home and moderation abroad, the Jeffersonian Obama administration seeks a quiet world in order to be able to focus attention on domestic reform, which has always been President Obama's primarily political agenda. The administration strategically aims to reduce America's costs abroad – financial and human – by limiting US commitments whenever possible and redirecting military expenditures toward meeting pressing democratic needs at home. Preferring disarmament agreements to military buildups and hoping to substitute regional balance-of-power arrangements for unilateral US force commitments around the world, the president promotes an orderly international society in which burdens are shared and the military power of the United States is a less prominent feature on the international scene (Mead 2010).

Politics and policies: empowerment and burden-sharing to advance national interests

In order to advance these goals, Obama considers the most significant strategic challenge facing the United States in the decades ahead to be making the world's rising powers stakeholders in the global economic and political order. This view is rooted in an understanding of global peace and stability as more likely with some degree of great-power cooperation with powers such as Russia and China (Zakaria 2008). Accordingly, Obama has made significant efforts to strengthen the collaboration with the world's emerging powers through initiatives such as the New Strategic Arms Reduction Treaty, signed with Russia in April 2010; the expansion of US engagement with China and institutions such as the Association of Southeast Asian Nations (ASEAN); bilateral work on issues including food security, human rights, clean energy, and global inequality with Brazil; and the acknowledgment of India's "instrumental role ... in world affairs, international commerce, and global peace and security" (Blake 2011). The Obama administration's approach to collective action is reflected in Secretary Clinton's statement on the US's relationship with China: "We think the more our people learn to cooperate and collaborate, the more China and the United States will be able to find solutions to many global challenges."

This approach of empowerment and burden-sharing through cooperation has been prevalent in Obama's administration since he entered office. At a press conference on 10 July 2009 in connection with the G8 summit in L'Aquila, the president stated:

> Ultimately, this summit and the work we've done here reflects a recognition that the defining problems of our time will not be solved without collective action. No one corner of the globe can wall itself off from the challenges of the 21st century or the needs and aspirations of fellow nations. The only way forward is through shared and persistent effort to combat threats to our peace, our prosperity and our common humanity wherever they may exist.
>
> (Obama 2009)

In order to generate support and exert influence through cooperation, an ability to listen to different views; understand the various motivations; and focus on commonalities rather than differences has been central to Obama's foreign policy. The 2010 National Security Strategy document calls for more global engagement and seeks to counter fears that the US is at war with Islam. It avoids the Bush era controversy over language such as the phrase "global war on terror" and references to "Islamic extremism," adding that the "United States is waging a global campaign against al-Qaida and its terrorist affiliates. Yet this is not a global war against a tactic – terrorism, or a religion – Islam." While recognizing that countries will have diverging interests, Obama suggests that "they are more likely to want to cooperate than not cooperate" (Scherer 2009). As part of this strategy, Obama has sworn off the Bush practice of punishing foreign misbehavior by quickly cutting off diplomatic ties or threatening to end direct conversation. This was evident when, weeks after the bloody crackdowns began in Iran in 2009, the president said he still hoped Iran's leaders would meet with him at the negotiating table to discuss Iran's nuclear program.

Critics have been inclined to view this strategy as portraying an administration too eager to apologize for America's failings and too willing to surrender the nation's role as a single, indispensable superpower. Among them is former senior adviser to American Presidents Nixon, Ford, and Reagan, Pat Buchanan (2009), who has criticized the Obama administration for weakening United States' foreign relations, arguing that Obama is "ceding moral high ground to regimes and nations that do not deserve it." Obama defends his strategy as one reflective of a recognition of the world as it is, ending an era of illusion in which Washington was perceived to confuse projecting power with achieving results (Sanger 2010). Transitioning toward a stronger emphasis on soft power, Hillary Clinton suggests, "We are no less powerful. ... We are shifting from mostly direct application and exercise of American power [to an indirect approach]." Obama's foreign policy has consequently been described among supporters as "a form of realism unafraid to deploy American power but mindful that its use must be tempered by practical limits and a dose of self-awareness" (Dionne 2009). This new exercise of power requires patience and partners, and gets results more slowly (Clinton, cited in Sanger 2010). Blending the idealism of Obama's campaign with the realities of a volatile and threatening world, the National Security Strategy document describes a United States "hardened by war" and "disciplined by a devastating economic crisis." "In a world like this," Clinton continues, "American leadership isn't needed less. It is needed more. And the simple fact is that no global problem can be solved without us." As part of this effort, the National Security Strategy document insists, "we will maintain the military superiority that has secured our country, and underpinned global security, for decades."

While this collaborative approach has generated a widespread perception – both domestically and internationally – of President Obama as a liberal willing to compromise national goals for collective solutions, his stated intent is to develop relations with the purpose of advancing America's core security interests. This approach is both rooted in and reinforcing the state as a pluralist moral actor and its accompanying limited notion of moral responsibility in international affairs. Throughout his discourse, Obama reiterates that the purpose of collaboration is to advance "common interests and ... common values" (Blake 2011). Beyond the physical security of American people, this strategy relies on an interpretation of safety to also include American values and ideals.

Obama's Jeffersonian expansion of Bush's freedom agenda

Defining security more broadly than his predecessor did, Obama expands Bush's freedom agenda while drawing on the Jeffersonian tradition of cutting back on military spending to promote domestic democratic ideals. In 2006, George W. Bush explained, "We believe that people across the Middle East and across the world are weary of poverty, weary of oppression, and yearn to be free. And all who know that hope, all who will work and sacrifice for freedom, have a friend in the United States of America." Strategically placing political freedom in the context of economic freedom and development, Obama expands Bush's freedom agenda (Obama 2010). He speaks about preserving human dignity, enhancing people's economic prospects, and strengthening civil society. In language similar to that employed by his predecessor, Obama states:

> Born, as we are, out of a revolution by those who longed to be free, we welcome the fact that history is on the move in the Middle East and North Africa, and that young people are leading the way. Because wherever people long to be free, they will find a friend in the United States. Ultimately, it is that faith – those ideals – that are the true measure of American leadership.
>
> (Obama 2011a)

Similar to George W. Bush, therefore, Obama draws on the Thucydidean understanding of the US being safer in a world of similar states: "We have done so because we know that our own future is safer and brighter if more of mankind can live with the bright light of freedom and dignity" (*ibid.*).

However, unlike the Jacksonian-inspired approach of the Bush administration before him, the Obama administration has taken a different approach to the promotion of these ideals. Rather than increasing military engagement abroad, Hillary Clinton has repeatedly stressed the importance of reducing the budget deficit to sustain American power, arguing that American commanders and diplomats see the long-term national debt as one of the largest threats to American influence and to the country's ability to project power abroad (Sanger 2010). Compared with the relatively optimistic vision of George W. Bush, who sought to remake whole parts of the world under the banner of American moral authority, Obama thus brings a more conservative, cynical view to the question of when nations should act on ideological impulses to promote American values and ideals. President Obama believes that change most effectively happens over time and as a result of empowerment of people to determine their own destiny. In this view, the purpose of aid must be "to create the conditions where it's no longer needed – to help people become self-sufficient, provide for their families, and lift their standards of living" (Obama 2009). And while recognizing the important role of the United States in promoting "universal values" globally, President

Obama commonly refers to men like Dean Acheson, George Kennan, and Reinhold Niebuhr, all of whom were imbued with a sense of the limits of idealism and American power to transform the world (Zakaria 2008). Referencing Niebuhr (cited in Dionne 2009), President Obama warns that some of "the greatest perils to democracy arise from the fanaticism of moral idealists who are not conscious of the corruption of self-interest," and that a "nation with an inordinate degree of political power is doubly tempted to exceed the bounds of historical possibilities."

Yet, despite his hesitation to guide the process too aggressively, the Obama administration is optimistic about the world going their way: as nations develop, they become more modern and enmeshed in the international economic and political system. To Obama, countries like Iran and North Korea are holdouts against the tide of history. America's job, therefore, is not to impose its views or form of governance on other countries (Scherer 2009), but to push these progressive forces forward, using soft power more than hard, and to try to get the world's great powers to solve the world's major problems (Zakaria 2008). Advancing this process, President Obama presents himself internationally as he does domestically; as an embodiment of meritocratic achievement that can happen in free and open societies, encouraging the people of the world to take ownership of the political processes in their home countries.

The Obama administration asserts that it takes nothing away from America's extraordinary position in the world when they say that the US will not always lead in the efforts to promote these ideals (Scherer 2009). The president argues, "while the use of force is sometimes necessary, we will exhaust other options before war whenever we can, and carefully weigh the costs and risks of action against the costs and risks of inaction." And when it is necessary, he adds, "we will seek broad international support." Accordingly, in response to questions about how to resolve the potential conflict between respecting state sovereignty and intervening to defend the human rights of oppressed people, Obama has shown reluctance to step into a strong leadership position. He contends, "The threshold at which international intervention is appropriate, I think, has to be very high. ... There has to be strong international outrage at what's taking place. It's not always going to be a neat decision" (cited in Scherer 2009).

Acknowledging critics who "argue that there are many places in the world where innocent civilians face brutal violence at the hands of their government, and America should not be expected to police the world," Obama suggests that since Washington cannot intervene "wherever repression occurs, we must always measure our interests against the need for action." In this context, Obama has laid out the pluralist conditions under which, during his presidency, American troops would be called upon for military intervention:

> As Commander-in-Chief, I have no greater responsibility than keeping this country safe. And no decision weighs on me more than when to deploy our men and women in uniform. I have made it clear that I will never hesitate to use our military swiftly, decisively, and unilaterally when necessary to defend our people, our homeland, our allies, and our core interests.
>
> (Obama 2011a)

This also includes "times ... when our safety is not directly threatened, but our interests and values are." Stating that "the United States must reserve the right to act unilaterally if necessary to defend our nation and our interests, yet we will also seek to adhere to standards that govern the use of force," Obama expands the Bush Doctrine to justify pre-emptive action against threats, not only to safety, but also to American values and commercial interests.

Domestic support

By taking a centrist approach to foreign policy – fending off conservative attacks by promising that his withdrawal from Iraq will be "responsible" and that he will do "everything" to stop Iran from acquiring nuclear weapons – Obama has managed to gain a rare bipartisan consensus on foreign policy. Throughout his presidency he has gained support from both sides by winding down the war in Iraq; escalating the conflicts in Afghanistan and Pakistan; negotiating with Iran (although this has been more controversial); renewing efforts to broker peace between Israel and Palestine; and seeking warmer relations with Russia and China (McManus 2009). Obama's approach to Afghanistan in particular – sending in additional troops, while calling for their withdrawal beginning in July 2011 – reflects a sober compromise in an attempt to reconcile his administration's Jeffersonian worldview with the weight of inherited problems demanding Wilsonian engagement (Mead 2010). Throughout his speeches, President Obama reiterates his desire for domestic collaboration in the execution of foreign policy decisions, affirming that he acts after consulting with his "national security team, and Republican and Democratic leaders of Congress" (Obama 2011b).

Beyond the Obama administration's diplomatic approach, however, the distraction of the economic crisis and the battle over healthcare – issues where partisanship remains stronger – have contributed to turning heated debate into silence during President Obama's time in office. This silence has been exacerbated by the Republican exhaustion on foreign policy. The traumas of the Bush administration left them a legacy in need of "refreshment and rebranding" (Mead 2010). However, these needs have been postponed by the economic crisis, as in a recession, the Republicans know they need to win voters back on home economics first. Accordingly, due to his middle-ground approach and the distractions related to the recovery process after the Bush era, the Obama administration has faced less opposition to foreign policy in Congress than otherwise could have been expected.

The Obama administration has thus found itself in a unique position to implement a coherent and consistent foreign policy. However, as the case on Libya reveals, despite the administration's perceived commitment to a solidarist expanded notion of moral responsibility in international relations, the Jeffersonian Obama administration utilized this opportunity to recreate the identity of the state as a pluralist moral actor with an accompanying limited notion of moral responsibility in international affairs. Yet, aware of its solidarist commitments, the Obama administration underscores that there exists a moral responsibility to protect while encouraging others to effectuate this obligation. The following relational constructivist analysis illustrates how the US's practical and discursive response to Libya both contributed to reaffirming the continued dominance of a pluralist understanding of the state as a moral actor while advancing a solidarist commitment within the constraints of a pluralist world.

Libya

We just want to be able to live like human beings.
(Libyan civilian, cited in Obama 2011c)

Within weeks of the initiation of the upheavals in Libya in February 2011, the UN Security Council responded, providing the first seemingly consistent implementation of a solidarist expanded notion of moral responsibility in discourse and action. From the beginning of the crisis, the UN prioritized the protection of the Libyan population, reflected in Security Council Resolution 1970 (unanimously passed 15–0) and Resolution 1973 (UN Security Council 2011a, 2011b). Initially pressuring Gaddafi through diplomatic efforts and the imposition of economic sanctions, Gaddafi's forceful response generated escalated measures on behalf of the international community, including the implementation of a no-fly zone and air strikes to protect civilians, orchestrated by NATO. Representing a turning point in the response to mass atrocities, the debate within the United Nations was not on whether, but how to best protect civilians from mass atrocities. The international community's swift and decisive response was perceived as a demonstration of UN member states' prioritization of civilian protection and the acknowledgement of their commitment to the expanded notion of moral responsibility enshrined in the Genocide Convention (UN 1951) and the R2P. Despite the optimism engendered by these events, however, this study shows that there is little about the US or international response to Libya that indicates that the pluralist–solidarist tension generating inconsistent responses to human rights atrocities is resolved. By evaluating the practical measures and moral justifications of the US government in response to the upheavals in Libya, this case unpacks how the pairing of commonplaces served to reinforce the twofold pluralist and solidarist commitment of the state as a moral actor on the international scene.

Background: escalating violence and the United Nations' response

Libya was under the dictatorial leadership of Colonel Muammar Gaddafi since he seized power in a coup overthrowing King Idris in 1969. The unrest sweeping through Tunisia and Egypt in late 2010 and early 2011 generated open revolts against Gaddafi's dictatorship in several cities in Libya. Three days after the fall of Egyptian President Hosni Mubarak, on 14 February 2011, calls went out on Facebook for peaceful demonstrations against Gaddafi's 41-year reign. Initiated by a small nucleus of antigovernment opponents in Benghazi, it quickly spread, generating a forceful response by Colonel Gaddafi who dispatched the army to crush the unrest. On 21 February, Gaddafi's regime warned demonstrators that if their protests did not subside, the country could fall into civil war. The following day, Gaddafi gave an hour-long speech in which he blamed America for his problems, compared his own people to rats, and promised to show "no mercy" in inflicting punishment on the protestors. Colonel Gaddafi said he would rather die a martyr than step down, summoning his supporters to attack and "cleanse Libya house by house" until the protesters surrendered. Within the first six weeks of the conflict, several thousand people were killed and more than 335,600 displaced (Collins *et al*. 2011), escalating the protests into a bloody battle for territory between government and rebel forces.

The uprising in Libya – reported as the bloodiest to date against a long-term ruler in the Middle East – caused a domestic and regional humanitarian crisis. The response from the international community was instant, swift, and firm. Immediately following Gaddafi's speech on 21 February, the UN Secretary-General's Special Advisers on the Prevention of Genocide and the Responsibility to Protect issued a press statement (UN 2011c), expressing concern over "reports of mass violence coming from the Socialist People's Libyan Arab Jamahiriya." The statement warned, "if the reported nature and scale of such attacks are confirmed, they may well constitute crimes against humanity, for which national authorities should be held accountable." Invoking the language of the Genocide Convention and the R2P to attribute responsibility to the Libyan government to protect the citizens within its care, the Special Advisers "remind the national authorities in Libya … that the heads of State and Government at the 2005 World Summit pledged to protect populations by preventing genocide, war crimes, ethnic cleaning, and crimes against humanity, as well as their incitement." Following this statement, the UN Human Rights Council (UNHRC) met on 25 February, opening a Special Session on "the situation of human rights in the Libyan Arab Jamahiriya" (UNHRC 2011). The UNHRC subsequently adopted Resolution S-15/2, calling for the Libyan government to cease all human rights violations; for the UNHRC to establish an international commission of inquiry; and for the General Assembly to suspend Libya from the Council.

On 26 February, the UN Security Council unanimously adopted Resolution 1970, imposing an embargo and financial sanctions on Gaddafi and his family. Relying on an understanding of the state as a moral actor responsible for the protection of the citizens within its care, Resolution 1970 expressed "grave concern" over the situation in Libya, "deploring the gross and systematic violation of human rights, including the repression of peaceful demonstrators, expressing deep concern at the deaths of civilians, and rejecting unequivocally the incitement to hostility and violence against the civilian population made from the highest level of the Libyan government." Calling on the Government of Libya "to meet its responsibility to protect its population," the Security Council demanded an immediate end to the violence and action to address the legitimate demands of the population, including through national dialogue. They called upon the Libyan authorities to act with restraint, to respect human rights and international humanitarian law, and to allow immediate access for international human rights monitors and humanitarian agencies. Failing to meet these demands, the UN Security Council suggested that the legitimacy of the Gaddafi government would be in jeopardy. The Resolution referred Libya's crackdown on rebels to the International Criminal Court (ICC) for investigation into reports of crimes against humanity.

Over the next few days, as the fighting in Libya intensified, sanctions imposed by the international community broadened. The US froze more than $33 billion of the Gaddafi regime's assets. Further, joining with other nations at the United Nations Security Council, the US imposed an arms embargo and travel restrictions on Gaddafi and his advisers (Obama 2011a). On 1 March, in response to UNHRC Resolution S-15/2, the UN General Assembly unanimously suspended Libya's membership of the UNHRC, and on 3 March, the Prosecutor of the ICC, Luis Moreno-Ocampo, launched an investigation "following a preliminary examination of available information" (ICC 2011). However, rather than relinquishing power in response to this initial pressure from the international community, Gaddafi intensified his efforts to crush the rebellion. As France moved to recognize the Libyan National Council – the nascent rebel body claiming to provide an alternative to the Gaddafi government – as the legitimate representative of Libya's people, Gaddafi's forces sent warplanes to bomb Brega, extending attacks deeper into the rebel-held territory in eastern Libya (Reuters 2011b). The UN Secretary-General subsequently appointed former Foreign Minister of Jordan, Abdelilah Al-Khatib, to the position of special envoy to Libya on 5 March in an effort to address the humanitarian crisis and prepare for a transition of power.

Providing the foundation for further international dialogue on measures to protect civilians, the African Union (2011) denounced on 10 March the violence in Libya as "a serious threat to peace and security in that country and in the region as a whole, as well as to the safety and dignity of Libyans and of the migrant workers ... living in Libya." The African Union called for the creation of a High-Level Committee on Libya to engage with all parties and facilitate dialogue, rejecting any form of military intervention. Similarly, the Arab League initially took a strong position against the use of force by the Gaddafi regime, while suspending Libya from the League and calling for the imposition of a "no-fly zone." In an extraordinary session on 12 March, they

called on the Security Council to bear its responsibilities towards the deteriorating situation in Libya, and to take the necessary measures to impose immediately a no-fly zone on Libyan military aviation, and to establish safe areas in places exposed to shelling as a precautionary measure that allows the protection of the Libyan people and foreign nationals residing in Libya, while respecting the sovereignty and territorial integrity of neighboring States.

(Arab League 2011)

On 16 March, as Colonel Gaddafi's troops advanced to within 100 miles of Benghazi, announcing that "everything will be over in 48 hours," the United Nations Security Council passed landmark Resolution 1973, calling for an immediate cease-fire, a no-fly zone over Libya, and authorizing "all necessary measures" – referring to military action – to protect civilians against Gaddafi's army. The comprehensive Resolution reiterates "the responsibility of the Libyan authorities to protect the Libyan population and reaffirming that parties to the armed conflicts bear the responsibility to take all feasible steps to ensure the protection of civilians," warning that "the widespread and systematic attacks … may amount to crimes against humanity." Immediately following this meeting, Secretary-General Ban Ki-moon issued a statement, highlighting the historic decision achieved by the Council and his expectation for immediate action. The Secretary-General (UN 2011a) declared that Resolution 1973 "affirms clearly and unequivocally, the international community's determination to fulfill its responsibility to protect civilians from violence perpetrated upon them by their own government."

Two days after the Resolution was adopted, on 19 March 2011, American and European forces began a broad campaign of strikes against Colonel Gaddafi and his government, unleashing warplanes and missiles in a military intervention on a scale not seen in the Arab world since the Iraq war (Chulov *et al.* 2011). The purpose, as stated by Rice, was to engage "in a broad range of actions that will effectively protect civilians and increase the pressure on the Gaddafi regime to halt the killing and to allow the Libyan people to express themselves in their aspirations for the future freely and peacefully." On 24 March, the US announced that they were transferring command and control to NATO, whose mandate remained limited to the no-fly zone, although it could also act in self-defense, in cooperation with other states in the wider coalition. NATO assumed responsibility for the UN-mandated mission on 27 March (NATO 2011), stating that it "will implement all aspects" of Security Council Resolution 1973 "to protect civilians and civilian-populated areas under threat from the Gaddafi regime."

Despite this significant international pressure, Gaddafi's government forces continued to attack rebels advancing with the support of foreign warplanes (Reuters 2011b). In his first public appearance following the initiation of the international airstrikes, Gaddafi announced to his supporters that "We will not surrender .... This assault ... is by a bunch of fascists who will end up in the dustbin of history." While declaring receptivity to a ceasefire and negotiations – provided NATO "stops its planes" – the war in Libya continued. In May, the ICC issued three warrants of arrest for Muammar Gaddafi, his son Said Al Islam Gaddafi, and the head of Libyan intelligence, Abduallah Al Sanousi, for "crimes against humanity" committed in response to the insurgencies during the first weeks of the conflict. In August, rebel forces engaged in a coastal offensive and took most of their lost territory, capturing the city of Tripoli on 21 August, celebrating the imminent end of Gaddafi's four-decade rule (CNN 2011). Nevertheless, Gaddafi continued to evade capture, leading the loyalists in a rearguard campaign (Tran *et al.* 2011). On 16 September, the United Nations recognized the National Transitional Council as the legal representative of Libya, formally replacing the Gaddafi government. Colonel Gaddafi remained at large until 20 October, when he was captured and killed attempting to escape from Sirte (Reuters 2011a). On 23 October 2011, the National Transitional Council declared the liberation of Libya and the official end of the war (Al Jazeera 2011).

Early warnings and the United States' practical response

The United States led the international support of the Libyan people's democratic aspirations in response to Gaddafi's brutal attacks by mobi-lizing a broad coalition and securing an international mandate to protect civilians (Security Council Resolution 1970 and 1973). Unilaterally and with its allies, the US implemented sanctions, estab-lished a no-fly zone and arms embargo. As part of the NATO-led coalition, the United States provided support to the mission to protect civilians and civilian-populated areas in Libya by engaging and assist-ing the opposition and addressing humanitarian needs emerging from the crisis. As of 9 June 2011, the US government provided $80 million to meet humanitarian needs inside and on the borders of Libya (Blake 2011). On 25 August, the UN Security Council's Libya Sanctions Committee approved a US proposal to unfreeze $1.5 billion of Libyan assets to be used to provide critical humanitarian and other assistance to the Libyan people.

As in the case of Darfur, the United States was quick to invoke the solidarist language of the Genocide Convention and R2P to denounce Gaddafi's brutal response to the insurgence. As the United States and the international community increased pressure on the Libyan leader to renounce power, US Ambassador to the UN, Susan E. Rice (2011) made clear that the United States and the international community could see only one choice for Gaddafi and his aides: step down from power or face significant consequences. As Gaddafi and his forces continued their advance in response to international pressure to relinquish power, Obama made the following announcement:

> At this point, the United States and the world faced a choice. Gaddafi declared that he would show "no mercy" to his own people. He compared them to rats, and threatened to go door to door to inflict punishment. In the past, we had seen him hang civilians in the streets, and kill over a thousand people in a single day. Now, we saw regime forces on the outskirts of the city. We knew that if we waited one more day, Benghazi ... could suffer a massacre that would have reverberated across the region and stained the conscience of the world.
>
> (Obama 2011a)

Offering some of the toughest rhetoric in international discourse, Rice (2011) described Gaddafi's denials of the atrocities against his own citizens as "frankly, delusional. ... It only underscores how unfit he is to lead, and how disconnected he is from reality." Praising the UN Security Council for its unanimous resolutions, Rice continued, "When the only way a leader can cling to power is by grossly and systematically violating his own people's human rights, he has lost any legitimacy to rule. ... This is about ... a regime that has failed to meet its responsibility to protect its own population." Together with Samantha Power, who already supported military intervention, and Secretary of State, Hillary Clinton, who came to support it, Rice overcame internal opposition from Defense Secretary Robert Gates, security adviser Thomas Donilon, and counterterrorism adviser John Brennan (Cooper and Myers 2011; Thrush and Negrin 2011).

In a complex political climate, UN Security Council Resolution 1973 provided the legal foundation for the US-led military intervention by the multi-state coalition in violation of Libya's sovereignty. Due to the sensitive nature of military action by the US against an Arab nation, the US sought Arab participation in the enforcement of a no-fly zone.

Moreover, cautious of being drawn into a potentially protracted and costly military campaign, the US quickly transferred command of the no-fly zone enforcement to NATO. Emphasizing that "these strikes will be limited in their nature, duration, and scope," Obama (2011d) explained that "their purpose is to support an international coalition as it takes all necessary measures to enforce the terms of UN Security Council Resolution 1973. These limited US actions will set the stage for further action by other coalition partners." The president continued, "United States military efforts are discrete and focused on employing unique US military capabilities to set the conditions for our European allies and Arab partners to carry out the measures authorized by the UN Security Council Resolution." The empowerment and burden-sharing approach to foreign policy discussed above thus characterized the US response to Libya:

> As the bulk of our military effort ratchets down, what we can do – and will do – is support the aspirations of the Libyan people. We have intervened to stop a massacre, and we will work with our allies and partners as they're in the lead to maintain the safety of civilians. We will deny the regime arms, cut off its supply of cash, assist the opposition, and work with other nations to hasten the day when Gaddafi leaves power. It may not happen overnight, as a badly weakened Gaddafi tries desperately to hang on to power. But it should be clear to those around Gaddafi, and to every Libyan, that history is not on his side. With the time and space that we have provided for the Libyan people, they will be able to determine their own destiny, and that is how it should be.
>
> (Obama 2011a)

Invoking the language of the Resolution, Obama argued that Gaddafi's attacks and threats against civilians and civilian populated areas "constitute a threat to the region and to international peace and security." Through the "illegitimate use of force," Gaddafi "has forfeited his responsibility to protect his own citizens and created a serious need for immediate humanitarian assistance and protection." The Obama administration thus relied on the pairing of commonplaces associated with the R2P to both delegitimize the Gaddafi regime and justify a forceful international response to the conflict.

Early warnings and the United States' rhetorical response: pluralist moral justifications

To justify the US-led intervention, President Obama deployed solidarist rhetoric emphasizing the importance of human rights as an element of US national interest and the role of the United States in leading the world on this important issue. Challenging the prevailing pluralist, limited notion of moral responsibility in international relations and the moral superiority of the United States driving the previous administration, President Obama related the experience of the people of Libya to that of Americans, drawing attention to Gaddafi's attacks on innocent civilians, hospitals, ambulances, and journalists, and quoting Libyan requests for freedom: "For the first time we finally have hope that our nightmare of 40 years will soon be over" (Obama 2011a). Comparing Benghazi to Charlotte, the president stressed the imminent threat of massacre, insisting, "It was not in our national interest to let that happen. I refused to let that happen" (*ibid.*). Linking US power to responsibility, while reasserting his expanded notion of the national interest to entail American values and ideals, President Obama continued:

> To brush aside America's responsibility as a leader and – more profoundly – our responsibilities to our fellow human beings under such circumstances would have been a betrayal of who we are. Some nations may be able to turn a blind eye to atrocities in other countries. The United States of America is different. And as president, I refused to wait for the images of slaughter and mass graves before taking action.
>
> (Obama 2011a)

Yet, aware of his pluralist primary commitment as president to the citizens of the United States, President Obama continuously relates his commitment to human rights to the national interest of the United States, confirming "why this matters to us." Emphasizing the United States' strategic interest in Libya, Obama proclaimed:

> America has an important strategic interest in preventing Gaddafi from overrunning those who oppose him. A massacre would have driven thousands of additional refugees across Libya's borders …. The democratic impulses that are dawning across the region would be eclipsed by the darkest form of dictatorship, as repressive leaders concluded that violence is the best strategy to cling to power.

The writ of the UN Security Council would have been shown to be little more than empty words, crippling its future credibility to uphold global peace and security. So while I will never minimize the costs involved in military action, I am convinced that a failure to act in Libya would have carried a far greater price for America.

(Obama 2011b)

He continues, in his letter to the Speaker of the House (Obama 2011d), "For these reasons, I have directed these actions, which are in the national security and foreign policy interests of the United States." In this way, President Obama unpacks the concept the national interest to reveal its combination of instrumental and humanitarian elements. Drawing on the rhetorical commonplaces of the Genocide Convention and the R2P to underscore that there exists a moral responsibility to intervene in Libya on humanitarian grounds, the Obama administration simultaneously emphasizes his primary responsibility as president to protect the lives and interests of the American people and encourages others to effectuate the obligation to intervene. In this manner, Obama strives to accommodate the administration's both pluralist and solidarist commitments. At the same time, it reveals President Obama's ability to consider and adapt his argument to various audiences.

Acknowledging the skepticism against US interventions abroad and the criticism that "the US should not be expected to police the world, particularly when we have so many pressing concerns here at home," Obama responds, "It is true that America cannot use our military wherever repression occurs. And given the costs and risks of intervention, we must always measure our interests against the need for action. But that cannot be an argument for never acting on behalf of what's right." Accordingly, in the case of Libya, President Obama justified intervention based on a unique set of circumstances:

In this particular country [Libya]; at this particular moment, we were faced with the prospect of violence on a horrific scale. We had a unique ability to stop that violence: an international mandate for action, a broad coalition prepared to join us, the support of Arab countries, and a plea for help from the Libyan people themselves. We also had the ability to stop Gaddafi's forces in their tracks without putting American troops on the ground.

(Obama 2011a)

By pairing rhetorical commonplaces in this way, the Obama administration's pluralist justification for the intervention in Libya
simultaneously served to respond to criticism of the administration's
inconsistent policy on humanitarian intervention as well as on relations
with the Arab world more broadly.

Naturally, questions have arisen as to why the United States chose to
intervene in Libya and not in Egypt, Yemen, Bahrain, or even Syria.
Despite the similarities between Libya and Syria, in particular, Obama
did not demand that Bashar al-Assad resigns following the intensifica-
tion of the Syrian government's bloody crackdown against the civilian
population on 29 April 2011. While stating that ignoring Libyans in
danger "would have been a betrayal of who we are," Obama made clear
that military action would not be "on the table" in Syria, where more
than 100,000 have been killed, and more than 2.5 million have fled the
country (Richter 2011). Instead, the United States has been pushing for
the transitional government called for in the Geneva communique and
backing Syria's "moderate opposition" with "non-lethal" assistance,
including communications equipment, generators, and office supplies
(*ibid.*).

The divergent American responses to the human rights violations in
Libya and Syria illustrate Obama's nuanced and focused approach to
foreign policy based on the starkly different national interest calculations the United States faces in these countries. Accordingly, Obama
makes clear that a number of different factors need to be taken into
account when considering the concept of the national interest and how
it relates to the government's commitment to the solidarist notion of a
responsibility to protect. Pronouncing that it is impossible to adopt a
single doctrine that fits each case, Obama's approach reinforces the
identity of the state as a pluralist moral actor in international relations.
It also reveals that part of the challenge in justifying the divergent
responses to these crises is related to the fact that it has less to do with
humanitarian issues than with harder calculations of national interest.

While the death tolls in Syria have continued to increase, they were
for a long time far lower than the numbers that were feared killed in
Libya. According to a senior official (cited in Richter 2011), they "were
not anywhere near the kind of situation that drew all the international
support for Libya." Moreover, although Libya is a major oil producer,
the strategic stakes were smaller in Libya than in Syria. Further, US officials worried that a collapse of the Syrian regime could lead to chaos that
could destabilize neighboring Lebanon and increase the risk of war with
Israel. They also feared that the secular dictatorship of President Bashar

Assad could be replaced by an Islamist government. Adding to the problems, Syria has deep sectarian divisions, which could crack open if the government's grasp was weakened. Yet, the problem of course, as pointed out by Daniel Kurtzer, former ambassador to Israel and adviser to Obama in the 2008 election (cited in Richter 2011), is that "there isn't anything that really separates what's happening in Libya from what's happening in Syria – nothing at all." Accordingly, he continues, the administration's attempt to separate the two policies "isn't going to work if people keep getting killed." Since the initiation of the crisis in Syria, much has happened, altering the Obama administration's relationship with Syria and the Middle East in general. Most significantly, the advancement of the Islamic State (IS) in Iraq and Syria has forced the United States to reconsider its non-engagement approach to Syria. Outlining a combination of actions required to destruct the IS, President Obama said that he would not hesitate to take military action in Syria, but indicated that this was not imminent (Crowley 2014). The troubling developments in the Middle East confirm the complexity associated with the concept of moral responsibility in international relations.

The US-led intervention in Libya, and Mr. Obama's discourse on the Middle East in general, discloses an administration striving to reconcile its pluralist and solidarist commitments. While reinforcing the state as a pluralist moral actor, primarily responsible for the protection of the lives and interests of American citizens, Obama simultaneously strives to uphold the US's commitment to the solidarist values embedded in the Genocide Convention and the R2P by working in coalition with others to effectuate this obligation.

Divergent domestic interests

Similarly to the two previous cases, domestic opinion on the US involvement in Libya has been ambiguous, with reactions ranging from support to criticism. On 1 March, the US Senate unanimously passed a non-binding Senate resolution (S. Res. 85), urging the UN Security Council to impose a Libyan no-fly zone and encouraging Gaddafi to step down. On 6 March, Congressional Leaders prodded the Obama administration for a more aggressive US response to Libya's increasingly brutal attacks on opposition groups, calling for a no-fly zone and other military measures. Senator John F. Kerry (D-MA), chairman of the Foreign Relations Committee, raised the possibility of bombing military airfields in Libya to deny the use of runways to Muammar Gaddafi's air force. Senators McConnell (R-KY) and McCain (R-AZ) also spoke in favor of US military involvement to keep Libyan warplanes grounded, arguing, "We can't risk allowing Gaddafi to massacre people from the air" (McCain, speaking on ABC News 2011).

These calls for action were not universal, however. Many policymakers on Capitol Hill assailed the US intervention in Libya as unconstitutional, suggesting that US involvement was tantamount to an act of war. In this view, President Obama usurped the Congress war making power established in Article 1, Section 8 of the US Constitution. Rep. Rob Paul (R-TX) and Rep. Dennis Kucinich (D-OH) were among the most outspoken opponents of the Administration's Libya policy on Constitutional grounds, arguing that Congress was not consulted before cruise missiles were launched against the Gaddafi regime (Lyman 2011). Also John Boehner, the Republican speaker of the US House of Representatives, warned President Obama that he would have to stop all US involvement in Libya or risk violating the War Powers Act because the president did not have congressional authorization for the operation (cited in Fifield 2011). The warning came as Democrats and Republicans in Congress increased their opposition to US involvement in Libya, with legislative moves to block funding and seize Gaddafi's assets increasing as war fatigue set in on Capitol Hill. On 3 June, the US House of Representatives passed H. Res. 292, stating that the "President has failed to provide Congress with a compelling rationale" for the military campaign in Libya, asserting that the "President shall not deploy, establish, or maintain the presence of units and members of the United States Armed Forces on the ground in Libya unless the purpose of the presence is to rescue a member of the Armed Forces from imminent danger." The Resolution gave the Administration 14 days to explain their strategy in Libya and to convince Congress that US interests justified engagement. Also Congress Resolution 51 was voted on the same day, cosponsored by Democrats and Republicans, ordering Obama to withdraw forces from Libya. This resolution failed 148–265, however its support by 87 Republicans revealed a party shifting toward isolationism. On 13 June, the Republican-dominated House voted 248–263 to deny funding for further involvement in Libya motivated by dissatisfaction with President Obama having launched the operations in Libya in March without seeking their approval. Furthermore, the House passed a resolution blocking the president from sending ground troops to Libya, calling for a detailed report on the US's military engagement there. A similar bill stopping an on-the-ground operation was introduced in the Senate (Fifield 2011).

To address dissatisfaction, the Obama administration arguably attempted to keep Congress "fully informed, consistent with the War

Powers Resolution." On 21 March, President Obama addressed the Speaker of the House, following the implementation of UN Security Council Resolution 1973, asserting that the decision to intervene in Libya was constitutional:

> [A]t my discretion, US military forces commenced operations to assist an international effort authorized by the ... UN Security Council and undertaken with the support of European allies and Arab partners, to prevent a humanitarian catastrophe and address the threat posed to international peace and security by the crisis in Libya.
>
> (Obama 2011d)

President Obama continued, "The United States has not deployed ground forces into Libya," but are "conducting a limited and well-defined mission in support of international efforts to protect civilians and prevent a humanitarian disaster." The president's justification coincided with his supporters' argument that the president was acting within his authority as Commander and Chief of the US armed forces. The War Powers Act cedes the president this authority. Further, despite the opposition's attempt to categorize US and international involvement in Libya as a conventional war against the sovereign nation of Libya, US officials maintained that the actions undertaken was defined as humanitarian intervention. Adm. Mike Mullen, chairman of the Joint Chiefs of Staff, argued, "We ... started yesterday limited operation and ... narrow in scope focused on humanitarian efforts protecting the civilians in Libya" (cited in Lyman 2011).

Furthermore, as on most foreign policy issues, public opinion on the US intervention in Libya remained split down the middle (PollingReport.com 2011). According to a USA Today/Gallup Poll in mid-April, Americans were evenly divided over the scope of the mission with 45 percent saying the US should limit intervention to enforcing a no-fly zone and weakening Libya's military, and 44 percent saying it should expand to include removing Gaddafi from power. In response to the latter critique, raised by those who wonder why President Obama did not from the outset take more forceful action to remove Colonel Gaddafi from power by taking his life, Obama (2011a) clarified that "the task that I assigned our forces ... carries with it a UN mandate and international support." Exceeding the mandate of UN Resolution 1973 (UN Security Council 2011b) would risk splintering the alliance. The consequences would likely entail having to put US troops on the ground. "The dangers faced by our men and women in uniform would be far greater. So would be the costs, and our share of the responsibility of what comes next" (Obama 2011a). Through this approach of burden-sharing and limited intervention, Obama responds to the ambiguity of public opinion surrounding the issue of intervention, reiterating that his highest priority is to protect American citizens by not putting American troops on the ground while underscoring a moral responsibility and encouraging other to effectuate this obligation. Aware of his audience, President Obama thus responds to divergent views among the American public; those critical of intervention as well as those promoting a more forceful response. Being able to make such humanitarian arguments, even while placating domestic concerns and justifying actions in the language of the national interest is significant. While firmly rooted in the pluralist Jeffersonian tradition, the US response to Libya therefore also reflects an effort to advance, however slightly, a solidarist commitment within the constraints of a pluralist world.

International pressure for action

In the case of Libya, the governments of France and Britain were, from the onset of the crisis, actively promoting a strong international response. Invoking rhetorical commonplaces affording action according to the R2P, British Prime Minister, David Cameron, argued that the military action against Gaddafi was "necessary, it is legal and it is right … because I don't believe that we should stand aside while this dictator murders his own people." President Sarkozy echoed this justification, saying "If we intervene on the side of the Arab nations it is because of a universal conscience that cannot tolerate such crimes" (Elliot 2011). However, as the above makes clear, more narrowly defined national interests play a significant role in determining international responses to prospective or ongoing mass atrocities. Despite the many speculations about why France and Britain were so eager to lead, the answer to this question remains unclear. Explanations related to trade, oil and gas, immigration, history, and personal profile remain at the level of specu-lation. Regardless of their motives, submitting to pressure to act by these powers, the US was able to present itself as an international leader strategically acting in collaborative ways through the UN and NATO to enforce US values and ideals.

Avoiding sole responsibility for another costly intervention, the Obama administration utilized practical and discursive approaches highlighting the US leadership role in international relations along with its multilateral approach to burden-sharing:

> In this effort, the United States has not acted alone. Instead, we have been joined by a strong and growing coalition. I'm ... proud that we are acting as part of a coalition that includes close allies and partners who are prepared to meet their responsibility to protect the people of Libya and uphold the mandate of the international community.
>
> (Obama 2011b)

In this context, President Obama makes clear that multilateralism can, while upholding the standards of the international community, simultaneously be utilized to promote more narrowly defined American interests abroad: "The burden of action should not be Americas alone. As we have in Libya, our task is instead to mobilize the international community for collective action." Unlike in the case of Darfur, the Obama administration worked in partnership with allies better equipped to undertake such a mission in response to the Libya crisis. Insofar as the Obama Administration emphasizes burden-sharing and placed some of that on others during the Libya operation, the approach substantiates the Bush rhetoric during Darfur: underscore the moral responsibility to act, but encourage others to effectuate the obligation. In this manner, the Obama administration may have succeeded in advancing a solidarist commitment within the constraints of a pluralist world.

Implications for the state as a moral actor

In the case of Libya, the international community, acting through the United Nations, redeemed its pledge to take "timely and decisive" action to "honor collective responsibility to protect people against atrocity crimes" in situations where governments were manifestly failing in their sovereign duty, unanimously agreed upon by world leaders in 2005 (Thakur 2011). The international community invoked the discourse of R2P and acted accordingly. According to Cohen, the intervention was done "right":

> ... with the legality of strong United Nations backing, full support from America's European allies, and quiet arming of the rebels. The Libyan people have been freed from a crazed tyranny. Unlike in Iraq, burdens were shared: America flew the intelligence missions

and did the refueling while the French, British, Dutch and others did most of the bombing.

(Cohen 2011)

Correspondingly, from a pluralist perspective, President Obama's leadership in response to the Libyan crisis was deemed "relatively extraordinary." Within 31 days of the initiation of the protests, he imposed powerful sanctions; froze a significant amount of Colonel Gaddafi's assets; secured a Security Council resolution; organized an international coalition; executed a limited military campaign; rolled Colonel Gaddafi's forces back to the west; took out the colonel's air defense; and debilitated much of his ground forces. All this was done without having to put American troops on the ground; without American military casualties; and with few Libyan civilian casualties. Moreover, with all this now done, America's own contribution could decline, NATO assumed command, and the European allies took on more of the burden. Compare that, say senior administration officials, to the years it took to intervene in Bosnia in the 1990s (Economist 2011).

Beyond the seeming success of the intervention in Libya, on 4 August 2011, the president issued Presidential Study Directive (PSD)-10 (White House 2011), on the creation of an Interagency Atrocities Prevention Board and corresponding interagency review. In the directive, advancing a solidarist perception of the state as a moral actor and an accompanying expanded notion of moral responsibility in international relations while maintaining focus on the protection and promotion of national interests, President Obama states that "Preventing mass atrocities and genocide is a core national security interest and a core moral responsibility of the United States." Motivated by a history which has taught us that "our pursuit of a world where states do not systematically slaughter civilians will not come to fruition without concerted and coordinated effort," the directive affirms that US security "is affected when masses of civilians are slaughtered, refugees flow across borders, and murderers wreak havoc on regional stability and livelihoods" (*ibid.*). PSD-10 continues, "America's reputation suffers, and our ability to bring about change is constrained, when we are perceived as idle in the face of mass atrocities and genocide." Acknowledging that the United States "still lacks a comprehensive policy framework and a corresponding interagency mechanism for preventing and responding to mass atrocities and genocide" (*ibid.*), President Obama established an interagency Atrocities Prevention Board with the primary purpose of coordinating prevention of mass atrocities and genocide. These efforts indicate an intent to seriously consider how the international community's solidarist commitment might be operationalized if many factors are met, including national interest considerations.

However, despite the optimism engendered by these efforts, the US response to Libya also clearly reveals the complexity of the plural-ist–solidarist tension generated by situations of severe human rights violations and the difficulties of upholding a state's both pluralist and solidarist commitments. Sadly, the current situation of human rights abuses and the advancement of IS in Syria and Egypt confirm the complexity of these situations. The US response to Libya – like the US response to Rwanda and Darfur – confirms that national interests continue to play a significant role in determining the lines of action taken by state leaders when confronted with situations of severe human rights violations. The problem, of course, is that, within the constraints of a pluralist world, we cannot avoid the question of whether it is real-istic to expect otherwise. As Obama declared in his Nobel Peace Prize address, as president, protecting the lives and interests of those he serve is his job.

From a solidarist perspective, the problem with celebrating the limited response to the human rights atrocities in Libya, is that overblowing the degree to which an expanded solidarist notion of moral responsibility has developed in international relations, does not neces-sarily advance the solidarist agenda. The fact that world leaders have been able to make humanitarian arguments, even while placating domestic concerns and articulating such arguments in the language of the national interest, is significant. Yet, within the context of the current international system, the distinction between nationals and foreigners ultimately generating inconsistent responses to situations of severe human rights violations remains strong. The Security Council press statement on Libya (UN 2011b) reiterates the distinction between "nationals" and "foreigners," highlighting the UN Security Council's "deep concern about the safety of foreign nationals in Libya." Similarly, throughout his statements, while recognizing a solidarist commitment to protect foreigners facing massacre, President Obama has been clear about his primary commitment toward the citizens of the United States: "First, we are doing everything we can to protect American citizens. This is my highest priority" (Obama 2011c). Looking back a few days into the conflict, Obama (2011a) said, "As president, my immediate concern was the safety of our citizens." From a solidarist point of view, this is clearly problematic, as it reinforces the constructed distinction between nationals and foreigners that they strive to eliminate. Failing to acknowledge and address this distinction, policy on humanitarian intervention will always risk being inconsistent and selective based on what is considered to be within the scope of the national interest.

References

ABC News (2011) Senator John McCain speaking to Christiane Amanpour on ABC's *This Week*, 4 March.

African Union (2011) African Union, Peace and Security Council Meeting, 265th meeting. 10 March. Available at www.au.int/en/sites/default/files/ COMMUNIQUE_EN_10_MARCH_2011_PSD_THE_265TH_MEETING _OF_THE_PEACE_AND_SECURITY_COUNCIL_ADOPTED_ FOLLOWING_DECISION_SITUATION_LIBYA.pdf (accessed 15 April 2011).

Al Jazeera (2011) NTC Declares "Liberation of Libya." 24 October. Available at www.aljazeera.com/news/africa/2011/10/201110235316778897.html (accessed 23 October 2011).

Arab League (2011) *The Outcome of the Council of the League of Arab States Meeting at the Ministerial Level in its Extraordinary Session on the Implications of the Current Events in Libya and the Arab Position.* 12 March. Available at http://responsibilitytoprotect.org/Arab%20League%20 Ministerial%20level%20statement%2012%20march%202011%20- %20english(1).pdf (accessed 15 March 2011).

Blake, Jr., R.O. (2011) Testimony before the House Foreign Affairs Committee, Subcommittee on the Middle East and South Asia. 5 April. Available at www.state.gov/p/sca/rls/rmks/2011/160020.htm (accessed 19 January 2015).

Buchanan, P. (2009) The Anti-Reagan. 9 September. Available at http://townhall.com/columnists/patbuchanan/2009/06/09/the_anti-reagan (accessed 29 May 2011).

Chulov, M., Harding, L., and Borger, J. (2011) Street Fighting Rages in Tripoli as Gaddafi Loyalists Fight Rearguard Action. *The Guardian*, 25 August. Available at www.theguardian.com/world/2011/aug/24/fighting-tripoli- gaddafi-libya (accessed 13 September 2011).

CNN (2011) Who is Saif al-Islam Gadhafi? 21 August. Available at http://edition.cnn.com/2011/WORLD/africa/08/21/libya.saif.gadhafi.profile/ index.html?hpt=hp_t1 (15 September 2011).

Cohen, R. (2011) Score One for Interventionism. *New York Times*, 29 August. Available at www.nytimes.com/2011/08/30/opinion/30iht-edcohen30.html (accessed 19 January 2015).

Collins, N., Roberts, L. and Henderson, B. (2011) Libya as it Happened: March 23. *The Telegraph*, 24 March. Available at www.telegraph.co.uk/news/ worldnews/africaandindianocean/libya/8403057/Libya-as-it-happened- March-23.html (accessed 19 January 2015).

Cooper and Myers (2011) Obama Takes Hard Line With Libya After Shift by Clinton. *New York Times*, 18 March. Available at www.nytimes.com/2011/03/19/world/africa/19policy.html (accessed 4 April 2011).

Crowley, P.J. (2014) Viewpoint: IS Won't Be Destroyed without Syria Change. BBC News, 12 September. Available at www.bbc.com/news/world-us-canada-29168779 (Accessed 11 September 2014).

Dionne, E.J. (2009) The Obama Doctrine. *The Washington Post*, 16 April. Available at www.washingtonpost.com/wp-dyn/content/article/2009/04/15/AR2009041502902.html (accessed 19 January 2015).

Economist (2011) Sarkozy's Libyan surprise. *The Economist*, 14 March. Available at www.economist.com/blogs/newsbook/2011/03/france_and_libya (accessed 4 May 2011).

Elliot, M. (2011) Viewpoint: How Libya Became a French and British War. *Time*, 19 March. Available at www.time.com/time/world/article/0,8599,2060412,00.html (accessed 4 May 2011).

Fifield, A. (2011) Congressional Opposition Rising to Libya Role. *Financial Times*, 15 June 2011. Available at www.ft.com/intl/cms/s/0/fbc39a70-96ad-11e0-baca-00144feab49a.html#axzz1h4nJSNgo (accessed 10 August 2011).

ICC (2011) ICC Prosecutor to Open an Investigation in Libya. 3 March. Available at www.icc-cpi.int/NR/exeres/3EEE2E2A-2618-4D66-8ECB-C95BECCC300C.htm (accessed 29 July 2011).

Lyman, J. (2011) Congressional Opposition to US Libyan Involvement. *Journal of Foreign Relations*, 22 March. Available at www.jofr.org/2011/03/22/congressional-opposition-to-u-s-libyan-involvement/ (accessed 31 May 2011).

McManus, D. (2009) Obamas Bipartisan Moment on Foreign Policy. *LA Times*, 5 April. Available at www.latimes.com/news/opinion/la-oe-mcmanus5-2009apr05,0,6956077.column (accessed 3 April 2011).

Mead, W.R. (2010) The Carter Syndrome. *Foreign Policy*, 4 January. Available at http://foreignpolicy.com/2010/01/04/the-carter-syndrome (accessed 2 March 2010).

NATO (2011) Statement by NATO Secretary General Anders Fogh Rasmussen on Libya. Press release 036. 27 March. Available at www.nato.int/cps/en/natolive/news_71808.htm?mode=pressrelease (accessed 30 March 2011).

Obama, B. (2011a) Remarks by the President to the Nation on Libya. National Defense University, DC, 28 March. Available at www.whitehouse.gov/the-press-office/2011/03/28/remarks-president-address-nation-libya (accessed 4 April 2011).

—— (2011b) Remarks by the President on Libya. Available at www.whitehouse.gov/the-press-office/2011/03/19/remarks-president-libya (accessed 4 April 2011).

—— (2011c) President Obama Speaks on the Turmoil in Libya: "This Violence Must Stop." *The White House Blog*, 23 February. Available at: www.whitehouse.gov/blog/2011/02/23/president-obama-speaks-turmoil-libya-violence-must-stop (accessed 4 April 2011).

—— (2011d) Text of a Letter from the President to the Speaker of the House of Representatives and the President Pro Tempore of the Senate. 14 October. Available at www.whitehouse.gov/the-press-office/2011/10/14/letter-president-speaker-house-representatives-and-president-pro-tempore (accessed 19 January 2015).

—— (2010) Remarks to the United Nations General Assembly. 23 September. Available at www.guardian.co.uk/news/blog/2010/sep/23/unitednations (accessed 5 April 2011).

—— (2009) Press Conference by the President. US Press Filling Center, LAquilla, Italy. 10 July. Available at www.whitehouse.gov/the_press_office/Press-Conference-by-the-President-in-LAquila-Italy-7-10-09 (accessed 3 April 2011).

PollingReport.com (2011) Libya: CNN/ORC Poll. Available at www.pollingreport.com/libya.htm (accessed 25 August 2011).

Reuters (2011a) Gaddafi Killed as Libya's Revolt Claims Hometown. 20 October. Available at http://af.reuters.com/article/topNews/idAFJOE79J09O20111020 (accessed 23 October 2011).

—— (2011b) Timeline – Libya's Uprising Against Muammar Gaddafi. 4 April. Available at www.reuters.com/article/2011/04/04/libya-idUSLDE72K0KK 20110404?pageNumber=3 (accessed 4 May 2011).

Rice, S. (2011) Libyans Fearing Violence if They Speak Out. *CNN News.* Transcript available at http://edition.cnn.com/TRANSCRIPTS/1103/01/nwsm.01.html (accessed 2 April 2011).

Richter, P. (2011) Obama's Nuanced Foreign Policy Evident in Libya vs. Syria. *Los Angeles Times*, 1 April. Available at http://articles.latimes.com/2011/apr/01/world/la-fg-us-syria-20110401 (accessed 19 January 2015).

Sanger, D. E. (2010) New US Strategy Focuses on Managing Threats. *The New York Times*, 27 May. Available at: www.nytimes.com/2010/05/28/world/28strategy.html?adxnnl=1&ref=world&adxnnlx=1303394677-b2vaUEIcwNgiQ0S1zsBagw (accessed 13 May 2011).

Scherer, M. (2009) The Five Pillars of Obamas Foreign Policy. *The Times*, 13 July. Available at www.time.com/time/nation/article/0,8599, 1910057,00.html (accessed 13 May 2011).

Thakur, R. (2011) UN Breathes Life Into "Responsibility to Protect." *The Star*, 21 March. Available at www.thestar.com/opinion/editorialopinion/2011/03/21/un_breathes_life_intoresponsibility_to_protect.html (accessed 19 January 2015).

Thrush, G. and Negrin, M. (2011) Barack Obama on Libya: Mission is "Focused." Available at www.politico.com/news/stories/0311/51561.html (accessed 1 April 2011).

Tran, M., Gabbatt A., and Haynes, J. (2011) Libya and the Middle East: Thursday 31 March 2011 Part One. *The Guardian*, 31 March. Available at www.guardian.co.uk/world/blog/2011/mar/31/libya-middle-east-syria-gaddafi (accessed 2 April 2011).

UN (2011a) Secretary-General, in First Report to Security Council on Libya

Situation Tells of Strong Diplomatic Efforts by the United Nations. 24 March. Available at www.un.org/News/Press/docs/2011/sgsm13475.doc.htm (accessed 2 April 2011).

—— (2011b) Press Statement on Libya. 22 February. Available at www.un.org/News/Press/docs/2011/sc10180.doc.htm (accessed 5 April 2011).

—— (2011c) Libya: Ban Welcomes Security Council Authorization of Measures to Protect Civilians. 18 March. Available at www.un.org/apps/news/story.asp?NewsID=37809&Cr=Libya&Cr1 (accessed 29 April 2011).

—— (1951) Convention on the Prevention and Punishment of the Crime of Genocide. Adopted by Resolution 260 (III) of the UN General Assembly, 9 December 1948. UN Treaty Series no. 1021, 78(277). Available at www.preventgenocide.org/law/convention/text.htm (accessed 6 September 2009).

UNHRC (2011) 15th Special Session on the "Situation of Human Rights in the Libyan Arab Jamahiriya." 25 February. Available at www2.ohchr.org/english/bodies/hrcouncil/specialsession/15/index.htm (accessed 29 July 2011).

UN Security Council (2011a) Peace and Security in Africa. Resolution 1970, S/RES/1970. 26 February. Available at http://daccess-dds-ny.un.org/doc/UNDOC/GEN/N11/245/58/PDF/N1124558.pdf?OpenElement (accessed 28 February 2011).

—— (2011b) The Situation in Libya. Resolution 1973, S/RES/1973. 17 March. Available at http://daccess-dds-ny.un.org/doc/UNDOC/GEN/N11/268/39/PDF/N1126839.pdf?OpenElement (accessed 17 March 2011).

White House (2011) *Presidential Study Directive/PSD-10.* Washington, DC: Office of the Press Secretary, The White House. Available at http://responsibilitytoprotect.org/White%20House%20PSD.pdf (accessed 6 August 2011).

—— (2010) The National Security Strategy of the United States of America. May. Washington, DC: The White House. Available at www.whitehouse.gov/sites/default/files/rss_viewer/national_security_strategy.pdf (accessed 3 April 2011).

Zakaria, F. (2008) Obama, Foreign Policy Realist. Available at http://newsweek.washingtonpost.com/postglobal/fareed_zakaria/2008/07/obama_foreign_policy_realist.html (accessed 8 April 2011).

5   Responsibility to whom?

Armed humanitarian interventions raise problems related to the issue of "self-determination" and "state sovereignty," established in Article 2(4) and described as "the corner-stone of the UN Charter" (Brownlie 1981: 699). Yet, the prerogatives of sovereignty eroded considerably during the second half of the twentieth century, creating new space and opportunities for legitimate humanitarian action. With this, article 1(1) of the UN Charter, referring to the maintenance of "international peace and security" has been reinterpreted to include security beyond the state. Numerous agreements, including the formal and unanimous adoption of the Convention on the Prevention and Punishment of the Crime of Genocide (UN 1951) and the doctrine known as the responsibility to protect (R2P) (ICISS 2001) confirm that "state sovereignty" does not exist without limits by strengthening the foundation for collective responses to situations of genocide, war crimes, ethnic cleansing, and crimes against humanity.[1] Nevertheless, the international community repeatedly fails to respond adequately to atrocities, turning the pledge of "never again" into a mockery of itself.

In response to these inconsistencies, a body of literature has developed that is concerned with the question of whether a norm of collective moral responsibility in response to severe human rights violations has emerged. This research has been important in establishing the individual as the primary object of security in international relations. However, what this literature has largely failed to consider are the difficulties associated with this solidarist development for the governments of potential intervening countries, whose primary moral duty remains the protection of their own citizens.

This study has demonstrated that one of the problems inherent in current approaches to humanitarian intervention is their tendency to collapse individual and state morality. Acting on the ideological reservoir of the state, policy makers are at constant risk of losing moral authority by basing their decisions on precedence considerations in situations where their individual moral compass may not be compatible with state policy. The Rwanda case, in particular, clearly illustrates the personal and presidential challenges related to President Clinton's efforts to pursue a Jeffersonian foreign policy in an environment contesting the pluralist, limited understanding of the state as a moral actor associated with this tradition.

Beyond these ideological traditions, the conscience of individual national leaders, domestic public opinion, and international political dynamics play a considerable role in determining political behavior at the state level. Primary among the concerns guiding decisions about whether to intervene in prospective cases of humanitarian interventions are those related to the human and financial costs associated with such missions. The president has a particular responsibility to protect the lives and interests of the citizens of the United States and is accountable to the American people in situations in which he fails in this responsibility. As illustrated by this study, the difficulties confronted by the Clinton administration in justifying intervention in another African quagmire following the "Somalia disaster" significantly impacted the decision not to intervene in Rwanda.

The cases analyzed in this study further illustrate that fear related to how action or inaction may be perceived impact decision-making when confronted with situations of severe human rights violations. Domestically and internationally, prospective interventions may be perceived as motivated by a solidarist desire to protect innocent civilians from severe human rights violations or by a more pluralist desire to advance instrumentally defined national interests. Emerging in highly contested normative spaces, situations of human rights violations are consequently at constant risk of being accompanied by loud objections. This was the case in Kosovo, where NATO conducted what is largely considered a legitimate humanitarian intervention. Despite the legitimacy of the NATO mission, the intervention generated loud protests, causing hesitation with regard to perceptions in similar situations in the future.

Furthermore, decisions about whether to act in prospective cases of humanitarian interventions need to consider both the short-term and long-term consequences of an intervention. Questions related to whether there exists a reasonable chance of success has haunted the intervention in Afghanistan and clearly impacted the Obama administration in connection with the intervention in Libya. Furthermore, as evidenced in Rwanda in particular, the US administration operates within an environment of intense and convoluted pressure, complicating the president's ability to determine which crises demand response at a given time. Beyond the complexity surrounding decision-making on armed intervention illustrated in this study, more multifaceted elements related to the institutional structure within which state leaders operate further constrain moral decision-making powers.

Due to the moral complexity of state leadership, therefore, this book contends that the moral stance of policy-makers must be separated from the moral stance of individuals. Yet, this is not to suggest that the complexity of statecraft excuses inaction in response to situations of genocide. On the contrary, it argues that an international community serious about the pledge of "never again" must address this complexity in order to avoid continued inconsistencies in response to mass atrocities.

As Machiavelli (1984: 93) asserts, "it must be understood ... that a prince ... cannot observe all of those virtues for which men are reputed good, because it is often necessary to act against mercy, against faith, against humanity, against frankness, against religion in order to preserve the state." In order to secure consistent responses to situations of severe human rights violations, therefore, the unique ethical sphere of statecraft must be addressed. In contrast to (among others) Luck (2008: 14), suggesting that "domestic sovereignty ... need not pose a barrier, legally or politically" to humanitarian intervention, this study demonstrates that it is precisely in the moral duty of state leaders to protect the lives and interests of the people which they govern, that the primary obstacle to consistent responses to severe human rights violations lies. Subsequently, the development of more complex agreements reiterating our common responsibility in situations of grave human rights violations with the hope of resolving the issue of inconsistent responses to such atrocities are in danger of repeating past mistakes as they fail to address the flawed assumptions of existing approaches. As the cases in this study show, while the identity of the state as a moral actor and the notion of how far moral responsibility extends in international relations have been challenged significantly in recent decades, fundamental contradictions inherent in the international system continue to generate inconsistent responses to situations of severe human rights violations, demanding attention and reassessment.

This book proposes that the controversy surrounding the concept of humanitarian intervention in recent decades is reflective of an international community striving to reconcile its pluralist and solidarist foundations. Arising from a wide range of social, political, economic, and technological forces, a solidarist consciousness has developed in international relations, making a retreat to pluralist state-based conceptions of international order and justice impossible. However, as the cases in this study show, attempts to move towards promoting a more consistent and coherent conception of global justice are constrained by the context in which they must develop, which remains heavily structured around pluralist mechanisms that reflect various types of inequality. This tension is reflected in the inconsistent US responses to the cases of severe human rights violations discussed in this study. In recent years, Williams (2005), Weinert (2011), Luck (2011), and others have presented compelling arguments, suggesting that what is needed is a "sovereign-sensitive" approach. Yet, from a solidarist perspective, such an approach is problematic because as long as we continue to accept that states will make decisions about humanitarian intervention not solely based on humanitarian concerns, without regard for political and cultural boundaries, we will continue to witness inconsistent responses to situations of severe human rights violations.

According to Morgenthau (1948), any movement away from a focus on the state as the primary object of security in international relations must be coupled, if not preceded, by a transformation at the level of the community. In concurrence with Morgenthau, this book suggests that in order to advance a solidarist expanded notion of moral responsibility in international relations, individuals must have shifted their primary allegiance from their local community to a world community (Little 2003: 449). In an environment demanding international engagement with moral questions across national boundaries, the state needs to be moved from a position of centrality to that of a component part within a larger whole, replacing the ethic of nationalism with an ethic of world citizenship.

Pluralists commonly invoke the argument that the notion of universal values or universal responsibility towards one's fellow human beings in the world does not have universal resonance. In the United States, especially among those commonly categorized as Jacksonians, these sentiments are tied to the notion of its "special providence" (Mead 2002). There are strong sentiments in the American population that the US constitution was God's gift to humanity. Depicting the Founding Fathers as divinely inspired individuals, W. Cleon Skousen's (1981) *The 5,000-Year Leap: A Miracle that Changed the World* currently inspires a large Tea Party movement defending what they consider to be an endangered US Constitution (Luce 2010). The Tea Party movement and other branches of conservatism in the US today share important characteristics with other fundamentalist movements. To these groups, the US

Constitution is arguably viewed as akin to a new set of 10 command-ments of God's chosen people. It is consequently not negotiable (Wolfgram 2010). The problem with this fundamentalism – as with other fundamentalisms – is that there is no dialogue to be had with those outside the movement of "true believers" (*ibid.*). On the contrary, it generates paranoia against the outside world. This has significant impli-cations for US foreign policy. According to Cerny (2010), the US's post-immigrant population has always seen the United States as differ-ent from – and superior to – the rest of the world. Such movements fear that increasing international involvement will erode America's excep-tional place in the world. This trend by many governments, groups, and individuals espousing ideologies, including ethnic or religious national-ism, favoring membership in a specific group over humanity as a whole lays down a direct challenge to a solidarist expanded notion of moral responsibility in international relations.[2]

The solidarist response to these arguments highlights how human society's "circles of empathy" have steadily expanded throughout the course of human history, from an initial kernel of family and friends, to the tribe, the city state, and the nation. This phenomenon has been rein-forced in recent times by ever-growing international mobility and communication across political and cultural boundaries. In this view, the significance of borders in situations of grave human rights violations is not in accordance with the most basic principle of morality – the protection of humanity as such, as this is manifested in all people. At the heart of Wilsonianism, this perspective entails a moral duty on behalf of the United States to protect and promote human freedom across the world. However, as the cases in this study suggest, in a society that is still strongly influenced by the Hobbesian notion of human nature, any attempt at advancing norms based on cosmopolitan values needs to consider the underlying assumptions of contemporary Western society.[3]

While increasingly contested (Boulding 1990), the conventional wisdom within many of the social sciences throughout the twentieth century has been that "human nature" is essentially selfish and adver-sarial.[4] This view strongly informs the structures and practices of modern society. Throughout the contemporary public sphere, contest, competition, confrontation, and other adversarial expressions, struc-tures, and practices are considered the norm (Karlberg 2004).[5] As evidenced by the continued failure to respond effectively to situations of mass atrocities, inherent to this adversarial environment is the dynamic that there will always be a "winner" and a "loser." This will inevitably lead to compromises which may not be in the best interest of the whole, since victory is sought rather than a favorable result that also utilizes the insights and resources of the "loser." While some processes leading to winners and losers are admittedly legitimate in a well-regulated market setting, as long as all participants to the race are treated fairly (as in a "perfect" market system, with full knowledge and equal rules for all), it seems that this same adversarial structure can have detrimental effects when applied uncritically in the wrong settings. If, in dealing with situations of genocide and mass atrocities, we persist in understanding human beings largely in economic terms, as self-interested creatures whose satisfaction lies and should lie in material gain or competitive advantage, we easily defeat the purpose of the practice of humanitarian interventions.

As a normative ideal, the principle of free market competition was first articulated in its full form by Adam Smith ([1776] 1910), who outlined the theory of modern capitalism and provided a moral justification for the pursuit of self-interest, transforming it from a historical vice into a modern virtue. Smith, however, understood the pursuit of self-interest as the pursuit of an interest in underlying values, which need not be strictly materialistic. Thus, an enlightened and altruistic market actor might have an interest in bettering the conditions of his or her fellow citizens. In this sense, Smith's notion of competition may be compatible with the concept of cooperation for humanitarian purposes. Since Smith's time, however, theories of competition may be said to have done too little to cultivate the *non*-material interests that Smith assumed. Instead, a largely utilitarian and materialistic faith in the virtue of self-interested market transactions has arisen, and competition seems to have become an overarching value, even within practices where ideals of free-market competition make little sense. Within a system of adversarialism, as this study shows, there will always be the possibility – and an increasing one as corruption of various forms creeps into the system – that money or power will win out, with no tangible connection to the creation of justice.

The UN Security Council assumes that one of its primary functions is to negotiate conflicting interests within a society in a utilitarian manner that satisfies the widest possible range of those interests. The standard by which we tend to evaluate the decisions of the UN Security Council is therefore very similar to the standard by which we evaluate economic systems: how well they allegedly maximize the satisfaction of competing self-interests. Toward this end, the UN has been structured much like the capitalist free market. It is an arena within which state-representatives try to advance their particular ideals and interests in a self-interested and competitive manner (Briand 1999: 154). In this regard, despite its idealistic foundation, the UN system has largely evolved into an arena of "political entrepreneurship" that derives from the market model, representing competing ensembles of interests (Lyon 1992: 129). Thus, as illustrated by this study, while the mandated goals of protecting international peace and preserving human rights coincide at the level of the UN Security Council, competing individual state agendas dominate their discussions, serving to undermine the purpose of the organization. The question of whether the motives of the actors in the UN Security Council (both individuals and the governments they represent) can be reconciled with the altruism ideally guiding the organization in order to effectively promote human rights is thus of critical importance. As an immediate step in responding to this question, we must revive the discussion on global governance, collective security, and the establishment of an independent standing UN army to implement the decisions of the Security Council.

At the state level, this book demonstrates that, contrary to the common representation of politics and ethics as mutually exclusive spheres, "political action must be based on a coordination of morality and power" (Carr 1939: 97). Utilizing a relational constructivist approach to the study of the state as a moral actor in international relations, it illustrates the interplay between the two, highlighting the centrality of moral justifications to the attribution of power to the state to engage in humanitarian interventions. By pairing rhetorical commonplaces such as "situations of genocide" or "severe human rights violations" with a "responsibility to protect" and the "national interest," the US government affords itself the power to engage in humanitarian interventions. This social attribution of power simultaneously constructs the actor as legitimately able to perform the action in question, and legitimizes the action because this actor performs it. Legitimation processes thus serve to isolate certain activities, such as the Bush and Obama administrations did with regard to the humanitarian interventions in Darfur and Libya, and render them acceptable by characterizing them as activities of "the state." Conversely, by avoiding this same rhetoric, the state can legitimize inaction, as the Clinton administration did in Rwanda. Examining this process of legitimation in response to the human rights violations in Rwanda, Darfur, and Libya, this study contributes to our understanding of the complexity of moral decision-making at the state level.

Moreover, by analyzing the concept of power in this way – as something that is continuously created and recreated through a process of legitimation – this book contributes to our understanding of the concept of power itself. The concept of power is central to international relations. Yet, as pointed out by Barnett and Duvall (2005), disciplinary discussions tend to privilege only one form of power: an actor controlling another to do what they would not otherwise do. Whether utilizing military, economic, or soft power (Nye 2004), the concept of power has throughout history been largely interpreted in this manner; as an advantage expressed in terms of means to be used against others to confer on its beneficiaries the ability to acquire, to surpass, to dominate, and to win (Karlberg 2004). This interpretation of power has been an attribute especially associated with men rather than women (Brock-Utne 1989; Reardon 1996, 1994, 1993), and has become an inherent feature of a culture of division and conflict. In the culture of contest that has consequently emerged, people tend to be preoccupied not only with relations of power, but also to think and talk about power as though its exercise is inherently competitive and conflictual (Karlberg 2004). Given the fact that the ways we think and talk influence the way we act, this has significant social implications for relations among states and how the UN Security Council approaches decisions regarding collective responses to situations of severe human rights violations. Competitive and conflictual discourses of power provide a clear example of this as they translate into competitive and conflictual models of social practice, as highlighted by the dynamics within the UN Security Council when confronted with situations of mass atrocities. By showing conceptual favoritism, the discipline of international relations not only overlooks the different forms of power in international politics, but also fails to develop sophisticated understandings of how global outcomes are produced and how actors are differently enabled and constrained to determine their fates based on these assumptions.

Highlighting the interplay between power and morality in international relations, this study confirms Carr's (1939: 100–101) assertion that "power will, to the end of history, be an area where conscience and power meet, where the ethical and coercive factors of human life will interpenetrate and work out their tentative and uneasy compromises." As pointed out by Wendt (1999: 376), "[the] emergence of an international public sphere signals the emergence of a joint awareness, however embryonic at this stage, of how their [realists'] own ideas and behavior make the logic of anarchy a self-fulfilling prophecy." By highlighting the role that our practices play in sustaining social kinds, this constructivist analysis contributes to enhancing our collective capacity for critical self-reflection, helping us overcome the false sense of determinism that has dominated international relations for centuries by opening up for the possibility of thinking self-consciously about what direction to take in the future.

The normative solidarist agenda underlying humanitarian intervention is a political project. It will make a difference to the extent that it reflects – and is perceived to reflect – popular sentiments and values, across societies, borders, and regions. As the Secretary-General put it in his 2009 report on implementing the R2P (UN Secretary-General 2009: 27), "Across the globe, attitudes have changed in important ways since Cambodia, Rwanda, and Srebrenica, raising the political costs, domestically and internationally, for anyone seen to be blocking an effective international response to an unfolding genocide or other high-visibility crime." Yet, the need to distinguish the R2P as a principle and a guide to tactical issues remains problematic, because, as Luck (2011) points out, "it is one thing to be a compelling but largely theoretical concept and quite another to be tested in a most public way in some of the toughest life and death crisis of the day." Moreover, channeling moral rectitude into effective policy remedies is a formidable challenge. While the translation of moral indignation into multilateral policy instruments is underway, its integration into notions of national interests and hierarchies of national security priorities is bound be a long and difficult process (*ibid.*).

In this process, we must not forget the pivotal question: "responsibility to whom?" The evolution of the concept of humanitarian intervention indicates that there exists a responsibility on behalf of some actor or actors to protect innocent civilians from massacre in situations where the state fails in its responsibility to do so. This study has contributed to highlighting some of the complexities associated with this moral responsibility at the state level. The question we must ask ourselves is whether the complexity of considerations excuses inaction when confronted with situations of severe human rights violations such as in Rwanda in 1994, or in Syria today. This study illustrates that despite the universal agreement that "something must be done," we continue to accept excuses based on a pluralist limited understanding of moral responsibility to stand idly by while genocide unfolds. As pointed out by Power (2003: 510), unless US officials are held "publicly and professionally accountable for inaction" in response to genocide, their calculus will likely not be altered. When is an excuse good enough that we consider it acceptable? In an increasingly interconnected world, how do we expect state leaders to balance different moral responsibilities? Events of recent history suggest that these are questions that are likely to continue to be among the most fundamental questions of contemporary international politics – and among the greatest questions of morality as such. In addressing them, we must "refuse to accept despair as the final response to the ambiguities of history," in the words of Martin Luther King (1964). We must "refuse to accept the idea that the 'isness' of man's present condition makes him morally incapable of reaching up for the eternal 'oughtness' that forever confronts him" (*ibid.*).

Notes

1   The R2P advocates a reconsideration of sovereignty to include a dual responsibility: "externally – to respect the sovereignty of other states, and internally, to respect the dignity and basic rights of all people within the state" (ICISS 2001: 8, §1.35). According to the report, commissioned by the Government of Canada, a state must bear "the primary responsibility for the protection of its peoples." Moreover, should a state fail in this responsibility; either independently or in partnership with external actors, then "the principle of non-intervention yields to the international responsibility to protect" (*ibid.*: xi). This report thus asserts the notion of "conditional sovereignty," and a shift in the foundation of international dialogue from that of a "right to intervene" to a "responsibility to protect" a population within a state's care.

2   It should be added here that American Conservatism is multi-faceted, and that it also contains strains that are less inward-looking. The Neo-Conservative movement, and arguably President George W. Bush himself, have defended principles of international responsibility and the protection of human rights across borders (even if many of the actual actions undertaken to defend these principles have been highly controversial and have been seen by many as purely unilateral rather than solidarist). Such principles are viewed by Conservatives as consistent with, and supportive of, US strength and national interest, but not necessarily as merely instrumental. The Christian foundation of much of US Conservatism can be said to have contributed to these more international, even solidarist trends, as exemplified by the pressure to act in defense of human rights in Sudan, discussed earlier.

3   R.B.J. Walker's *After the Globe, Before the World* represents an important contribution towards this end, providing fertile ground for further research on these essential questions (Walker 2009).

4   The term adversarialism refers to the pursuit of mutually exclusive interests by individuals or groups working against one another. Contest, competition, and confrontation are all expressions of adversarialism (Karlberg 2004). The term *normative adversarialism* stems from Fellman (1998), who uses this term to refer to expressions of adversarialism that stem from conformity to popular cultural norms and can be consciously rejected by those who choose to do so. In contrast, Fellman uses the concept of *compulsive adversarialism* to refer to compulsive or addictive

expressions of adversarialism (i.e. deep psychic drives) that are beyond conscious control (Karlberg 2004).

5   There is, admittedly, also a plausible claim to be made for viewing competition as fruitful and dynamic. The idea of separation of powers combined with checks and balances found in the political philosophy of the *Federalist Papers* (Hamilton *et al.* [1788] 1982), for instance, is one that convincingly views self-interest not as being necessarily egoistic in a destructive or materialistic sense, but rather one that highlights the advantages of institutions and agencies attempting to secure their power and mandate, and thereby attempting to do their job in the best possible way, making sure other institutions or agencies do not overstep their boundaries. The mutual competition thus ensures both quality and a check on the power of others. No one institution or branch becomes all-powerful, and mistakes can more easily be corrected along the way. Most modern market theorists would hold the same view about an efficient market equilibrium: competition based on an interest in preserving one's own institution or corporation (or even oneself as an individual), and securing for it (or for oneself) more gain, is what encourages new ideas, improves and strengthens efforts, and ensures that resources are not wasted, but rather that the market place maintains a real orientation towards the needs of its users.

References

Barnett, M. and Duvall, R. (2005) Power in International Politics. *International Organization* 59(1): 39–75.

Boulding, K.E. (1990) *Three Faces of Power.* Newbury Park, CA: Sage Publications.

Briand, M. (1999) *Practical Politics: Five Principles for a Community that Works.* Chicago, IL: University of Illinois Press.

Brock-Utne, B. (1989) *Feminist Perspectives on Peace and Peace Education.* New York: Pergamon Press.

Brownlie, I. (1981) *Principles of Public International Law*, 6th edn. Oxford: Clarendon Press.

Carr, E.H. (1939) *The Twenty Years Crisis: 1919–1939.* London: Macmillan.

Cerny, P.G. (2010) Decline has Fuelled Paranoia and the Tea Party. *Financial Times*, 30 October: 12.

Fellman, G. (1998) *Rambo and the Dalai Lama: The Compulsion to Win and Its Threat to Human Survival.* Albany, NY: State University of New York Press.

Hamilton, A., Madison, J. and Jay, J. ([1788] 1982) *The Federalist Papers.* Toronto: Bantam Books.

ICISS (2001) The Responsibility to Protect: Report of the International Commission on Intervention and State Sovereignty. December. Ottawa: The International Development Research Centre. Available at http://responsibilitytoprotect.org/ICISSReport.pdf (accessed 13 January 2015).

Karlberg, M. (2004) *Beyond the Culture of Contest.* Oxford: George Ronald.

King, M.L. (1964) Nobel Peace Prize Acceptance Speech. Available at www.nobelprize.org/nobel_prizes/peace/laureates/1964/king-acceptance_en.html?print=1#.VHgww8m9aSo (accessed 28 November 2014).

Little, R. (2003) The English School vs. American Realism: a meeting of minds or divided by a common language? *Review of International Studies* 29: 443–460.

Luce, E. (2010) Taking America Back. *Financial Times*, 30 October. Available at www.ft.com/intl/cms/s/2/88143c46-e1e1-11df-b18d-00144feabdc0.html (accessed 19 January 2015).

Luck, E.C. (2011) The Responsibility to Protect: The First Decade. *Global Responsibility to Protect* 3: 1–13.

—— (2008) Sovereignty, choice, and the R2P. *Global Responsibility to Protect* 1(1): 10–21.

Lyon, V. (1992) Green Politics: Parties, Elections, and Environmental Policy. In R. Boardman (ed.), *Canadian Environmental Policy: Ecosystems, Politics, and Process*, 126–143. Toronto: Oxford University Press.

Machiavelli, N. (1984) *The Prince* (trans. D. Donno). New York: Bantam Books.

Mead, W.R. (2002) *Special Providence.* New York: Routledge.

Morgenthau, H. (1948) *Politics Among Nations.* New York: Alfred A. Knopf.

Nye, J. (2004) *Soft Power.* New York: Public Affairs.

Power, S. (2003) *A Problem from Hell: America in the Age of Genocide.* New York: Harper Perennial.

Reardon, B. (1996) *Sexism and the War System.* New York: Syracuse University Press.

—— (1994) *Learning Peace: The Promise of Ecological and Cooperative Education.* Albany, NY: State University of New York.

—— (1993) *Women and Peace: Feminist Visions of Global Security.* New York: State University of New York Press.

Skousen, W.C. (1981) *The Five Thousand Year Leap.* Malta, ID: National Center for Constitutional Studies.

Smith, A. ([1776] 1910) *An Inquiry into the Nature and Causes of the Wealth of Nations*, vol. 2. London: J.M. Dent.

UN (1951) Convention on the Prevention and Punishment of the Crime of Genocide. Adopted by Resolution 260 (III) of the UN General Assembly (9 December 1948). UN Treaty Series no. 1021, 78(277). Available at www.preventgenocide.org/law/convention/text.htm (accessed 6 September 2009).

UN Secretary-General (2009) Implementing the Responsibility To Protect. Report of the Secretary-General, A/63/677, 12 January. Available at http://responsibilitytoprotect.org/implementing%20the%20rtop.pdf (accessed 19 January 2015).

Walker, R. (2009) *After the Globe/Before the World.* London: Routledge.

Wendt, A. (1999) *Social Theory of International Politics.* Cambridge: Cambridge University Press.

Williams, J. (2005) Pluralism, Solidarism and the Emergence of World Society in English School Theory. *International Relations* 19(1): 19–38.

Wolfgram, G. (2010) Tea Party's Fundamentalist Passion Poses a Danger. *Financial Times*, 2 November: 12.

Index